Success with
Container
gardening
for large plants

H. AND D. MITTMANN

Series Editor
LESLEY YOUNG

D0334729

MEREHURST

Contents

Flowering plants from
southern climates

Most people would like to create
a little subtropical magic on their
balcony or patio by growing large
container plants with luxuriant
green leaves and beautiful
flowers in stylish containers.
In this guide, authors Helga and
Dieter Mittmann, who have had
many years of experience in
growing such plants, offer
advice on the successful care
of container plants and show
you how to create a "southern
hemisphere" paradise on your
balcony or patio. Easy-to-follow
tables provide tips on appropriate care during the summer and
winter months. Here you will find
advice about the care of all of the
most popular container plants
and also many splendid new
varieties and exquisite rarities.
All of the large container plants
originate from sunny southern climates and they will only manage
to survive the winter in temperate
climates if you learn how to care
for them properly. Drawing on
their many years of experience,
the authors are able to provide
answers to all of the most commonly asked questions about
overwintering – from moving
plants into their winter quarters
to the correct ways to care for
them and to prepare for the
new growing season. Clear and
detailed illustrations will help
even complete beginners to care
for these plants successfully.

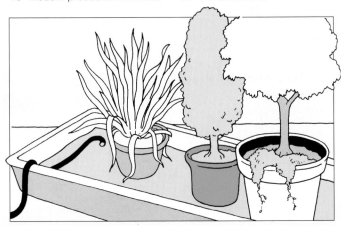

Short-term irrigation using a piece of permeable interfacing fabric.

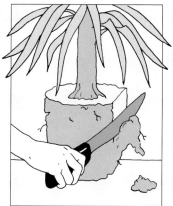

Reducing the rootstock.

Overwintering plants indoors.

The authors

Helga and Dieter Mittmann are the proprietors of a nursery that specializes in large container plants in Salzbergen, Germany. They also run a mail order business that sells young container plants and offers one of the largest selections of such plants in Germany. Their knowledge of the cultivation, care and overwintering of large container plants is based on many years of practical experience.

The photographers

Jürgen Stork has been working as a freelance photographer since 1982. His main areas of interest are fashion, advertising and nature. He has worked for many periodicals, including the popular German magazine *Mein schöner Garten*. This guide also contains photographs by other well-known plant photographers (see p. 62).

The illustrator

György Jankovics studied at the academies of art in Budapest and Hamburg, where he trained as a technical draughtsman. He has worked for many well-known publishing companies and is an outstanding illustrator of animal and plant subjects.

Important: Please read the Authors' note on page 63.

Purchasing and positioning

The secret of success with all plants lies in choosing the ideal position. Select the correct container plants for the right places on your balcony or patio and you will be well rewarded with a wealth of beautiful flowers.

From left to right: Bougainvillea glabra, Nerium oleander, Citrus limon, Hibiscus rosa-sinensis.

Purchasing and positioning

What are container plants?

When we think of large container plants, we usually conjure up an image of sunshine, sandy beaches, blue sea and exotic plants that flower profusely in the warm southern regions of the world. Such plants are usually unable to cope with frost, so they have to be kept in large containers in temperate climates. Of course, they cannot be treated as indoor plants either. By definition, large container plants are tough, long-lasting plants that live outside during the summer and spend the winter in a frost-free, well-aired place.

The parts of a plant

The root system anchors the plant firmly and supplies it with water and nutrients. The roots are adapted to the normal conditions of their natural habitat: that is they are wide-spreading (flat-rooting), deep-rooting (tap roots) or water-storing (tubers). The type of root system should, therefore, be taken into consideration when choosing a container (see p. 56).
The main axil from which the plant branches out determines its general appearance. It may form a stem with a crown (tree), produce many branches (shrub) or be leafy (herbaceous). The entire plant is filled with vascular

tissue, which transports water and nutrients from the roots to the leaves. Before buying any plant, the container gardener must first decide which plants (whether they are herbaceous, shrubs or climbing or hanging plants) will have enough room on the patio or balcony in question.
The leaves deal mainly with respiration, photosynthesis and the processing of nutrients. They come in an infinite variety of shapes and types, from the simplest green leaf to the leathery evergreen leaves of Mediterranean plants, from the delicate, sap-filled leaves from humid regions of temperate climates to the evergreen leaves of tropical plants and the water-storing leaves of plants from semi-arid regions.
The flowers contain stamens and ovaries, which function as reproductive organs. These are protected by petals, which can display an enormous range of colours and shapes, particularly among the tropical and sub-tropical species, and often have wonderful scents.
Often, one of the most important criteria for the collector of large container plants is to have a beautiful and, if possible, particularly longlasting display of flowers.
Lifespan: Plants usually survive for much longer when they are in their natural habitats rather than in large containers.

Plant names

In the field of botany, all plants bear Latin names; these are regulated through the "International Code of Botanical Nomenclature" (ICBN) and are recognized all over the world. The basic classification unit is a species. Groups of closely related species belong to one genus. A number of genera with similar characteristics are grouped in a family.
The name of an individual species comprises the generic name, e.g. *Punica*, and the species name, e.g. *granatum*. This may be followed by a cultivar or variety name, e.g. 'Nana', which is the dwarf pomegranate tree. Using common names only often leads to confusion as they may vary from region to region. For this reason, it is preferable to use the botanical name.
The names of families of plants (Punicaceae in our example) are always identifiable by their suffix -aceae. Knowing what family a plant belongs to will also provide information about its require-ments as to care or its particular mode of reproduction. Today, in addition to pure species, a large number of crosses exist. These are known as hybrids.

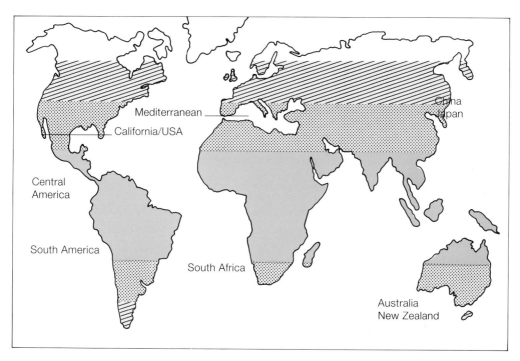

The countries of origin of large container plants

On holiday in warm countries such as Spain, Portugal or Italy, you may have been introduced to some of the large container plants, such as the heavenly *Nerium oleander*, the richly coloured bougainvillea or the splendid *Bauhinia*. This may lead you to suppose that these plants are native to these countries. However, they come mainly from the subtropics, where the summers are often hot and dry and the winters moist, cool and frost-free, except at high altitudes.

These climatic zones are shown in the map above. The shading provides the following information:
● diagonal hatching: temperate climate;
● dotted: subtropical climate;
● solid blue: tropical climate.

Plants and their origins
California, USA: *Campsis, Fremontodendron.*
Central America: *Asarina, Choisya, Fuchsia, Passiflora.*
South America: *Abutilon, Bougainvillea, Brugmansia, Cestrum, Erythrina, Iochroma, Mandevilla, Passiflora, Solanum, Tibouchina.*

Mediterranean areas: *Arbutus, Ceratonia, Cistus, Laurus, Myrtus, Nerium, Olea, Viburnum.*
South Africa: *Agapanthus, Anisodontea, Carissa, Leonotis, Plumbago, Podranea, Strelitzia.*
China and Japan: *Camellia, Citrus, Cycas, Eriobotrya, Lagerstroemia, Nandina, Nerium, Pittosporum, Punica, Trachelospermum.*
Australia and New Zealand: *Acacia, Callistemon, Corokia, Dodonaea, Eucalyptus, Hardenbergia, Leptospermum, Metrosideros, Pandorea, Phormium, Sollya.*

7

Left and below: Nerium oleander comes in double or single flowered forms. They are sensitive to rain.

Evergreen container plants

Right: Tibouchina urvilleana (princess flower).
Below: Calliandra tweedii (Indian paint brush).

During the winter, evergreen container plants require a bright, but not sunny, position as their leaves will continue the process of photosynthesis even during this cold season. The winter rest period merely triggers off a slower general metabolic rate. Of course, even evergreen plants do not retain the same leaves forever but will gradually replace them one by one, so do not be alarmed if your evergreens lose a leaf or two.

Left: Agave americana, (the American agave) will not flower until it is 30–40 years old.
Below: Trachelospermum jasminoides.

Above: Fremontodendron californicum is covered in large yellow flowers and will tolerate even very hard water.

Above: Passiflora 'Kaiserin Eugenie' is a particularly robust and large-flowering passion flower.

Above: Fortunella margarita (kumquat) is a citrus tree with plum-sized, glowing orange fruits that can be eaten, skin and all. There are several varieties with green and white or green and yellow foliage.

Purchasing and positioning

Name	Flowering time / Colour	Position	Watering / Fertilizing	Cutting back	Notes
Acacia species	XI–IV / yellow	○	medium (K)	R2/F	Bush/tree; scented; may cause allergic reaction
Acca sellowiana	V–VIII / white, red	○ ◐	frequently	R2	Bush; edible fruits; very attractive leaves and flowers; will benefit from cutting back
Agave americana		○	medium		Succulent; will live for a very long time; will need plenty of room as very thorny
Anisodontea capensis	III–XII / pink	○ ◐	frequently	R1/F	Bush; everlasting flowering; often artificially stunted; will tolerate "wet feet" during the summer
Arbutus unedo / strawberry tree	XI–III / white	○ ◐	medium (K)		Bush/tree; beautiful red strawberry-like fruits
Argyranthemum frutescens	IV–XI / yellow, white, pink	○	frequently	R1	Bush; remove faded flowers constantly; cut back during winter to avoid bare branches
Asarina erubescens	V–X / pink	○ ◐	frequently	R1	Climbing plant; long flowering time; produces lots of seed
Calliandra tweedii	IV–X / red	○	frequently	R2	Bush; can be grown on an espalier; some loss of leaves during winter; requires protection from rain
Callistemon species	IV–VII / red, yellow	○	frequently (K)	R2/F	Bush; some varieties flower twice yearly; keep in cool position during winter
Ceratonia siliqua	XI–IV / yellow, red	○	sparingly	R2	Bush/tree; flowers and fruits only on very mature specimens; attractive leaves; easy to care for
Chamaerops humilis / dwarf palm		○	medium-frequently		Tree; grows very slowly; very robust and easy to care for; thorny
Choisya ternata / Mexican orange blossom	II–VI / white	○ ◑	frequently	R2	Bush; scented; attractive even as a green plant
Citrus species / lemon, orange and others	I–XII / white	○	medium (K)	F	Bush/tree; scented; flowers and fruits simultaneously; partly thorny
Clianthus puniceus	III–V / red, pink, white	○	medium	R2	Bush; flowers only during low winter temperatures
Corokia species	II–V / yellow	○ ◐	frequently	F	Bush/tree; beautiful flowers; interesting foliage; berries
Correa species	XI–V / pink, green, other	◑	frequently	R2	Bush; profusion of flowers in late winter if overwintered in cool position
Eriobotrya japonica	XI–II / white	○ ◐	medium		Bush; large, felted leaves; flowers and fruits only in a conservatory position; requires protection from rain
Fremontodendron californica	III–X / yellow	○	sparingly	R1/F	Bush; profusely flowering, bright yellow; may irritate skin; likes chalky soil
Hardenbergia violacea	III–IV / lilac	○ ◐	medium	R1	Climbing plant; ideal as a hanging plant
Hibiscus rosa-sinensis	I–XII / red, yellow, other	○	frequently	R1/F	Bush; beautiful flowers; often stunted; requires protection from rain
Homalocladium platycladum	VI–VIII / green	○	frequently		Bush; interesting flattened branches with flowers and berries along the edge
Kennedia coccinea	IV–IX / light red	○	medium	R2	Climbing plant; looks good as an espalier and also in hanging baskets

○ = sunny; ◑ = semi-shady; ● = shady; ☠ = warning: plant or parts of the plant are toxic; (K) = dislikes chalk or lime soil.

Name	Flowering time Colour	Position	Watering Fertilizing	Cutting back	Notes
Lagunaria patersonii	V–X pink	○	medium		Tree; easy to care for and resilient
Lapageria rosea	VIII–II red, pink, white	●	medium		Climbing plant; extremely beautiful flowers with wax-like bells; rare; never cut back
Laurus nobilis bay laurel	III–V white	○ ◐	medium	F	Bush; grows very slowly, remove shoot tips often; culinary herb
Leptospermum species	IV–VII red, white, other	○	medium-frequently (K)	F	Bush; sensitive to waterlogging and drought
Mandevilla amabilis	VI–IX pink	○	medium	R1	Climbing plant; requires protection against rain; milky sap may irritate the skin
Metrosideros species	V–VII red	○	frequently (K)	F	Bush/tree; very beautiful flowers; avoid waterlogging
Nandina domestica ☠	III–VII white	○ ◑	medium (K)		Bush; toxic; simultaneous flowers and red berries; frost-hardy if planted out
Nerium oleander ☠	V–X pink, white, other	○	frequently	R2	Bush; toxic; requires protection against rain; prevent it from becoming bare by regular cutting back
Olea europea olive tree	VII–VIII white	○	medium	F	Bush/tree; interesting shape of growth, may also produce fruit
Pandorea jasminoides	I–XII white, pink	○	frequently		Climbing plant; everlasting flowering; can be grown on an espalier
Parkinsonia aculeata	IV–VI yellow	○	medium	R2	Tree; long, hanging branches; thorny
Passiflora species passion flower	IV–X blue, red, other	○	medium-frequently	R1	Climbing plant; some species lose their foliage; slightly scented
Phoenix canariensis canary date palm		○	medium-frequently		Tree; very easy to care for; requires lots of space; pointed leaves
Pittosporum species	III–V white, red	○ ●	frequently	R2	Bush/tree; decorative foliage; scented flowers
Polygala myrtifolia	I–XII pinkish–red, lilac	○	medium-frequently	R2	Bush; numerous flowers
Sollya heterophylla	V–XII blue	○	medium		Climbing plant; longlasting flowering time with small, blue, bell-shaped blooms; grow on an espalier
Strelitzia reginae	II–VIII yellow, blue	○ ◑	sparingly		Shrub; exotic flowers; the seedlings will not bloom for years; avoid waterlogging
Tibouchina urvilleana	X–IV lilac	◐	medium (K)	R1	Bush; sensitive to sunburn; velvety leaves, usually flowers in winter
Trachelospermum species	IV–X white, yellow	○ ●	medium-frequently		Climbing plant; scented flowers; foliage turns reddish if overwintered in a cool position
Trachycarpus fortunei Chinese windmill palm		○	medium-frequently		Tree; thorny; can stand a light frost
Viburnum tinus	IX–V white	○ ◑	frequently	R2	Bush; many large, decorative flower umbels; hardy if placed in a sheltered position
Washingtonia robusta petticoat palm		○ ◑	medium-frequently		Tree; will not cope with centrally heated air; thorny

R1 = should be cut back; R2 = can be cut back; F = shaping cut recommended.

Right and below:
Solanum rantonnetii
can also be trained into
a standard shape. It
has extremely beautiful
blue flowers.

Deciduous
container plants

Abutilon hybrids bear bell-
shaped flowers in shades
of red, orange and yellow.

Right: Senna corymbosa has golden yellow flowers from the last month of spring into the first month of winter.

Deciduous container plants are easy to overwinter if you follow a few important rules. When caring for such plants during the winter, you must be aware that the plants will not lose their leaves all in one go but gradually, over a longer period of time, so they will constantly be surrounded by dried-up foliage. This should be removed regularly, especially in the vicinity of the pot, otherwise the dead leaves may harbour fungi, possibly leading to an infestation.

Left: Brugmansia has white to apricot-coloured flowers that release a heady scent in the evenings.

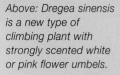

Above: Dregea sinensis is a new type of climbing plant with strongly scented white or pink flower umbels.

Above: Bougainvillea glabra and its varieties produce a profusion of glowing pinkish-violet flowers and are particularly robust.

Above: Plumbago auriculata bears masses of beautiful light blue flowers. The flowers need protecting from the rain.

Above: Punica granatum f. plena displays glorious double flowers but no pome-granate fruits, unlike the single-flowered species.

Purchasing and positioning

Name	Flowering time Colour	Position	Watering Fertilizing	Cutting back	Notes
Abutilon species	I–XII yellow, other	◐	frequently	R1	Bush; very easy to care for; everlasting flowering; seedlings often display new colours and shapes
Acnistus australis	IV–X white, blue	○ ◐	frequently	R1/F	Bush; everlasting flowering; grows fast; small bell-shaped flowers
Agapanthus species	V–X white, blue	○ ◐	frequently	—	Shrub; avoid waterlogging; definitely overwinter in a cool position
Albizia julibrissin	VII–IX pink	○	frequently	F	Tree; in the evening the leaves fold up
Araujia sericifera	VII–X white	○	frequently	R2	Climbing plant; the milky sap may start allergies or cause skin irritation; will trap insects at night
Asclepias curassavica	VI–IX orange	○	medium	R1	Semi-bush; spindle-shaped fruits
Bauhinia species	V–IX pink, white	○	medium	—	Bush; extremely beautiful orchid-like flowers
Bougainvillea glabra	V–IX lilac, other	○	frequently	R1	Climbing plant; prefers slightly acid soil; thorny
Brugmansia species ☠	V–X white, yellow, other	○	frequently	R1	Bush/tree; enchanting scent; will cope with any amount of cutting back; requires protection from wind
Caesalpinia gilliesii	V–VIII yellow, red	○	medium	R1	Bush; requires cutting back in order to form flowers
Campsis radicans trumpet vine	V–X yellow, red	○	frequently	R2	Climbing plant; large trumpet-shaped flowers; hardy in winter in a sheltered position; requires a wind-break
Cassia corymbosa	V–XII yellow	○	frequently	R1	Bush; easy-going, everlasting flowering; will cope with any amount of cutting back
Ceratostigma species	VI–X blue	○	frequently	R1	Bush/shrub; in the autumn, cut back to one hand's width; depending on the species, possibility of skin irritation
Cestrum species ☠	I–XII pink, red, yellow	○ ◐	frequently	R2	Bush; easy to care for, everlasting flowering; C. auranticum flowers in winter
Clerodendrum ugandense	IV–X blue	○	medium	R2	Bush; interesting flowers with long filaments
Cyphomandra betacea	III–VIII white, green	○	frequently	R2	Bush; fruits ripen during the winter
Diospyros kaki	V–VII yellow, white	○	medium	F	Tree; fruit-bearing plant, harvest the fruit in late autumn after the leaves fall
Dregea sinensis	III–X white, pink	○ ◐	medium-frequently	R1	Climbing plant; everlasting flowering; scented; requires large supply of nutrients; the milky sap will cause skin irritation
Duranta repens	V–IX blue	○ ◐	frequently	R2	Bush; thorny; beautiful flowers and yellow berries, flowers appear on the tips of the branches
Erythrina crista-galli	VII–X red	○	frequently	R1	Bush; thorny; requires no care during the winter; glowing red racemes
Ficus carica fig tree	—	○	frequently	R2	Tree; edible fruit; seedling plants will not bear fruit
Fuchsia hybrids	V–X	●	medium	R1/F	Bush; excellent for a north-facing position; a huge variety of flower shapes and colours

○ = sunny   ◐ = semi-shady   ● = shady   ☠ = warning: plant or parts of the plant are toxic; (K) = dislikes chalk and lime soil.

Name	Flowering time Colour	Position	Watering Fertilizing	Cutting back	Notes
Grevillea species	III–X red, white, other	○	medium (K)		Bush; needle-like leaves
Indigofera heterantha indigo bush	V–X blue	○ ◐	medium	R1	Semi-shrub; hardy in a sheltered position
Iochroma species	III–X lilac, red, other	○ ◐	frequently	R1	Bush; fast-growing and flowers while still a young plant; possible skin irritation; winter protection required
Jacaranda mimosifolia	II–V blue	○	medium	R2	Tree; hardly ever flowers in temperate climates
Juanulloa aurantiaca ☠	VII–XII orange	◐	medium	R1	Bush; interesting but slightly difficult to keep; the flowers almost never fully open up
Lagerstroemia indica	VIII–X pink, white, other	○	medium	R1	Bush/tree; will only flower during very good summers; requires protection from rain
Lantana hybrids ☠	IV–X many colours	○	frequently	R1/F	Bush; may become very old; easy to care for; thorny
Leonotis leonurus	VIII–XII orange	○ ◐	frequently	R1	Semi-bush; flowers late, but very colourfully
Leucaena glauca	V–X white	○	medium	R2	Bush; fine, feathery foliage; spherical flowers
Malvaviscus arboreus	XI–III red	○ ◐	medium	R1	Bush; flowers never completely open up
Mandevilla laxa ☠	VI–IX white	○ ◐	frequently	R1	Climbing plant; scented flowers; cut back almost to ground level; milky sap may cause skin irritation
Melia azedarach ☠	IV–VI violet	○	medium	R2	Tree; numerous flower umbels, berries; can stand cutting back
Montanoa bipinnatifida	I–III white	○	medium–frequently	R2	Bush; flowers better in a conservatory as the flower often forms rather late
Nicotiana glauca tobacco plant ☠	VII–IX yellow	○	frequently	R2	Bush; grows fast, easy to care for; self-sowing
Plumbago auriculata	VII–X blue, white	○	frequently	R1/F	Bush; the seedheads are sticky; branches break off rather easily; protect against wind and rain
Podranea ricasoliana	VIII–X pink	○	frequently	R1	Climbing plant; flowers very late
Poncirus trifoliata	IV–V white	○	medium	R2	Bush; hardy in a sheltered position; thorny
Punica granatum pomegrante	VI–X red, other	○	frequently	R1	Bush/tree; only the dwarf variety 'Nana' is everlasting flowering
Sesbania tripetii	V–X red	○	medium	R2	Bush; glowing panicles, remove seedheads; susceptible to mildew
Solanum species perennial nightshade ☠	III–XI blue	○	frequently	R1/F	Bush, climbing plant; everlasting flowering; *S. rantonnetii* is often stunted
Tecoma capensis	VII–X red	○	frequently	R1	Bush; grow as an espalier; will flower better outside than in a conservatory
Tecoma stans	V–X yellow	○	medium	R2	Bush/tree; loves plenty of light and warmth

R1 = requires cutting back; R2 = cutting back possible; F = shaping recommended.

Purchasing and positioning

Before you buy

The purchase of large container plants can turn out to be an expensive business, particularly if very large or rare plants are involved. It is worth considering the following points before buying so that your dreams of an exotic display of flowering plants do not turn into nightmares. You should take into account the plants' requirements as to position and amount of care and their full grown size and weight as well as storage problems during the winter.

Position

In the wild in their countries of origin, large container plants have adapted to the optimal conditions in their respective habitats. A knowledge of its botany (origins, habitat, family, etc.) will give you valuable information about the conditions a plant will require throughout the seasons. Climatic conditions and access to light in the position in which a plant is kept (garden, balcony, patio) are decisive factors. The closer these conditions approximate to conditions in their natural habitats, the more splendidly your container plants will grow and flourish. Also, consider the requirements of plants in respect to light, temperature and space where winter quarters are concerned (see p. 52).

Choosing the right position

Container plants for sunny positions

Sunny positions are those in which plants will benefit from sunlight all day long. You will need to water more frequently in sunny sites, but try to avoid watering plants at midday in bright sunlight. Young plants should always be protected from direct sunlight.
● Suitable plants:
Agapanthus, Albizia, Brugmansia, Caesalpinia, Ceratostigma, Citrus, Erythrina, Eucalyptus, Ficus carica, Fremontodendron, Homalocladium, Lantana, Nandina, Nerium, Passiflora, Phormium tenax, Plumbago, Punica granatum, Senna, Sollya, Strelitzia, Tecoma capensis.

Container plants that will also flourish in semi-shade

Semi-shady positions are mainly found on the west- or east-facing sides of a house where plants will only be exposed to sunlight for half the day or a few hours.
● Suitable plants:
Abutilon, Acca sellowiana, Anisodontea, Arbutus unedo, Asarina, Cestrum, Choisya, Correa, Corokia, Dregea sinensis, Duranta, Eriobotrya, Hardenbergia, Jasminum, Leonotis, Mandevilla laxa, Metrosideros, Tibouchina, Viburnum.

Container plants that will also flourish in the shade

Shady positions are not dark gloomy spots but such places as the north-facing side of a house or under open-crowned trees.
● Suitable plants:
Aucuba japonica, Camellia, Crinodendron, Fatsia japonica, Fuchsia, Lapageria rosea, Laurus nobilis, Pittosporum, Trachelospermum.

You will find further information on pages 10, 11, 14 and 15.

Plants for indoors at cool or warm temperatures

The determining factor for distinguishing between these two groups of plants is the minimum temperature that the plant needs the whole year round. The general rule is:
Cool indoor plants should be kept in a frost-free environment during the winter at temperatures of approximately 5–10° C (41–50° F). The majority of the best-known large container plants belong in this category.
Warm indoor plants require temperatures of more than 20° C (68° F) all year round and very high humidity, for example *Cyperus papyrus, Passiflora quadrangularis, P. coccinea, Senna didymobotrya* and *Thunbergia grandiflora.*
These plants can only be kept successfully in a heated conservatory or greenhouse.

Bougainvillea glabra forms massive flowering hedges in its subtropical countries of origin.

Bougainvillea.

Care

If you are a beginner, growing large container plants for the first time, you should choose plants that are relatively easy to care for and will give you few problems, e.g. *Brugmansia, Cestrum, Erythrina, Plumbago, Punica.* These plants will even cope with drought for short periods of time, do not react sensitively to every mistake made when watering, are not very susceptible to infestation by pests and can be overwintered with a minimum of care (see Plants for people who are out all day, p. 22).

Purchasing and positioning

Size and weight

Large container plants can develop into splendid bushes and trees, which can lead to problems, particularly in respect to the space they require on a balcony and in their winter quarters – just imagine trying to move them! If you have only a limited amount of space, you should choose plants that will tolerate pruning or do not grow very large. The tables on care (see pp. 10–11, 14–15) will give you relevant information.

Cost

The prices of large container plants vary a lot, depending on where you live and on their size, species, origins, availability and method of culture. As a rule, the most well-known and easily grown container plants are the most economical, such as *Abutilon, Bougainvillea, Cestrum, Nerium oleander* and *Tibouchina*, as they are "mass-produced". Young plants are also cheaper than more mature ones. Most imported, rare or "difficult" plants tend to be more expensive. A collector may be able to purchase a few rarities at reasonable prices among the plants imported or grown by specialist dealers.

Our tip: Toughen up these plants (and all plants that come straight from a greenhouse) by placing

Checklist when choosing plants

Position: What conditions (climate, amount of light) can you provide?
Shape of growth and height: Will the plant require a lot of space and will it tolerate cutting back?
Winter quarters: Have you enough space in a cellar or garage with the right amount of light, ventilation and temperature or do you have a greenhouse?
"Cool or warm" indoor plants: Are you able to provide the necessary conditions for these plants, even in winter?

Susceptibility to infestation by pests: Is the plant resistant to pests or does it attract them?
Dangers: Do children and/or pets have access to your house or garden? If so, avoid plants with thorns, and those that are toxic or can cause skin-irritation.
Flowers: Are you interested only in longlasting flowering times and scents? Is the plant summer- or winter-flowering? If it is kept in a cellar in winter, you will not have much luck with a winter-flowering plant.
NB: Please read the Authors' note on page 64.

them initially in a slightly shadier position outside, which is sheltered from the wind. In general, the most expensive specimens are large or old container plants as well as certain very rare plants.

Where to obtain container plants

You should be able to purchase the more commonly grown container plants from most nurseries, garden centres or even some of the larger supermarkets. If you are looking for something rarer, however, you will have to seek out specialist nurseries, many of which often also supply plants by mail order. Further possibilities are buying from, or swapping rare plants with, other hobby gardeners.

The following points should be considered:
● Always buy plants from a reputable nursery and, if possible, choose plants that were actually grown there.
● Find out whether the plants were grown from seed or cuttings. Plants propagated from cuttings are true to their variety and will flower earlier and better.

● Listen to specialist advice.
● Find out if you can continue to obtain specialist advice after purchasing the plant.

The range of container plants

When purchasing large container plants, remember that they are distinguished by price and size. Young plants are generally offered as cuttings or seedlings brought on in the same season or from the previous year. They are more reasonably priced but smaller than ready-grown plants. The advantage is that you can carry on growing them in your own garden under your own care. The disadvantage is that you will have to wait longer until they have attained a good size and they will need more care and overwintering.

As a rule, ready-grown plants are older and ready to flower. Some varieties will, however, flower at a young stage or grow very fast. Make sure you check the stem and branches: the more woody they are (you can tell by the light brown bark) the older the plant. The disadvantages of ready-grown plants are that they often find it more difficult to adapt to new conditions and they are also considerably more expensive.

Checklist when purchasing plants

Buying a healthy plant is the main prerequisite for good growth, a profusion of flowers and safe overwintering.

1. The structure of the plant: The stem and branches should be properly woody, display an attractive shape and have no broken bits. The total appearance of the plant should indicate that it has been well cared for.

2. Compost: This should be flower compost. It should not be too hard or wet and must be free of weeds. It should never be pure peat.

3. Roots: A well-developed rootstock, with white roots inside but not underneath the pot. Black or "glassy"-looking roots are a sign that they have died.

4. Foliage: Vigorous shoots, bright green in colour, lighter-coloured young leaves. No damage to leaves and no pests (look underneath the leaves). A residual coating on the leaves cannot be avoided, however, if watering, leaf fertilizing or spraying have been carried out, as some preparations leave a residue.

Modern production methods and their consequences

Today, plants are produced faster and more cost-effectively than ever in order to get them to the consumer as soon as possible. Because of the extent of the competition between different growers, this can now only really be achieved by the use of technical and chemical aids. As a general rule, plants are expected to propagate and grow quickly and flower profusely at the time of sale.

Production methods
● Fast growth is obtained by using extremely large amounts of fertilizer, so that the plants will look "market ready" in the minimum amount of time.
● The flowering time is accelerated by the use of special flowering fertilizers.
● Once the desired height of growth is achieved, any alterations in the general appearance of the plant are radically limited by means of chemical growth inhibitors, i.e. the plant is artificially stunted.
● The agent used for stunting the growth will simultaneously cause some plants to produce a greater number of flowers.
● Plants may be planted in specially adapted compost so that they can draw up and process large amounts of water and fertilizer more easily.

Purchasing and positioning

Abutilon loves a semi-shady spot in a secluded part of the garden.

Hand-finished clay pots.

● Cultivation often takes place in sealed units under "artificial" conditions, which generally means in greenhouses with automatic irrigation, ventilation and fertilization.

● In order to cope with the problems of pests that inevitably arise during mass culture procedures, massive doses of pest control agents are employed to protect the plants.

Consequences

● Because the plants are accustomed to an artificially sterile greenhouse climate, they will not have toughened up sufficiently and will have problems adapting to normal fertilizing and watering, as well as to a position outdoors.

● Certain insecticides lose their effectiveness, since the pests become resistant to them.

● The plant compost is geared to automatic irrigation or fertilizing rather than manual ways of watering and feeding.

● The stem and branches remain green in the autumn, which means they have not turned woody as they should and so will dry out during the winter.

● Stunted plants always develop problems during over-wintering. Many will have died by the following spring.

What to do when problems arise

Usually, it is not until some time after purchasing the plant, for example when you are ready to move it indoors for overwintering, that you realize you have a problem. Various measures may be undertaken to alleviate different kinds of damage.

Forced plants

Recognizable by immature wood (stem and branches are still green) and shoots that are too soft, particularly in the case of fast-growing plants like *Brugmansia* or *Iochroma*. Other characteristics include flowers that are larger than normal, e.g. in *Abutilon*, or very thin stems in the case of trees with crowns, e.g. *Anisodontea, Lantana* and *Solanum rantonnetii.*

Remedy: Do not stand the plant in bright sunlight, cut back rigorously (see p. 42) and stop

fertilizing so that the wood has a chance to mature before removal to winter quarters.

Overfertilized plants

These are recognizable by a short flowering time with a profusion of flowers, followed by excessive loss of leaves.

Remedy: Cut back rigorously, do not fertilize and water sparingly until new shoots appear.

Stunted plants

Usually recognizable by small stature and compact growth, unnaturally small leaves and an extreme profusion of flowers (e.g. *Anisodontea capensis, Solanum rantonnetii*).

Remedy: hardly possible; you can only wait until the effects of the stunting have grown out. This often takes several years.

Transportation of large container plants

Any kind of transportation is stressful for plants. However, if the journey is a short one and the plants have been properly packed up, they should not come to any harm.

Smaller plants should be placed standing upright in a container (a box, carton or basket) with enough packing to prevent them from falling over.

Larger plants should be transported upright or lying down, depending on their size

and dimensions. Avoid breaking off branches by pulling a bin bag or something similar over the plant. If this is not available, you can always tie the branches together without harming the plant if it is to be transported in your car. If it is to be transported lying down, it is a good idea to wrap the pot and rootstock in newspaper or to put the pot in a plastic bag or sack and tie it up.

By mail or other method: If large container plants are trans-ported by mail or rail, the plant should be thoroughly watered beforehand and secured against breakage by inserting bamboo sticks through the rootstock. Secure the compost in the pot by means of paper and adhesive tape. Further protection is provided by using a firm enveloping material for the entire plant, including its pot, and filling out the spaces with padding to prevent any breaking of branches or any other damage.

After purchasing

Once your plants have arrived, you should give them the best possible conditions right from the start, so that they can recover from the stress of being trans-ported and begin to adapt to their new habitat.

Purchasing and positioning

Plants for people who are out all day

Being in full-time employment, which takes you away from home most of the day, does not mean that you have to give up the idea of growing large container plants, providing you make sure to choose the right kinds of plants. A very wide range of large container plants can actually manage on very little care or overwintering. Make sure, therefore, that you choose your plants according to how much time you have for watering, fertilizing, etc. and, finally, the time you actually have to enjoy the beauty of their flowers. If you do this you will find out that, in spite of a full-time job, you will still be able to indulge your passion for large container plants.

The most suitable plants are those that:

● can cope with a short period of drought;
● will not mind an occasional mistake in watering;
● are not susceptible to attack by pests;
● are relatively problem free and can be overwintered with a minimum of care;
● create very little mess (falling leaves etc.).

This general information covers such plants as:

Agapanthus, Agave, Arbutus unedo, Bougainvillea, Calliandra, Choisya ternata, Corokia,

What to do when your new plants arrive

Step 1: Carefully unwrap the plant and check its appearance.

Step 2: Plants whose roots are growing out of the bottom of the drainage hole should be repotted after two to three days. This will occur more often in the case of mail order plants which have probably been kept for sale in the same sized pots for an entire season or have been kept in small pots to cut down on weight. Before repotting, water them thoroughly!

Step 3: If the rootstock looks dried out, submerge the plant in a bath of water until small bubbles are no longer seen to rise (see illustration, p. 31).

Step 4: Always place the plant in a slightly shady place that is sheltered from the wind so that it can acclimatize.

Step 5: Do not fertilize any new plants for at least two weeks, until they have adapted to their new environment. This will avoid the risk of overfertilizing.

Step 6: Cut back any long, thin shoots by about two thirds.

Step 7: Constantly check the further development of any new acquisitions. As a rule, after a week or so the plant will have recovered from being transported and can be placed in its final position.

Dodonaea, Eriobotrya, Ficus carica, Fremontodendron, Homalocladium, Jasminum, Lagunaria, Laurus nobilis, Nandina, Nerium oleander, Olea europaea, Parkinsonia, Pittosporum, Plumbago, Punica granatum, Sollya, Strelitzia, Trachelospermum.

Bringing home plants as holiday souvenirs

The importation of any plant is subject to a number of rules and customs regulations concerned with import duty, the transportation of pests and diseases and the protection of native species of plants. An infringement of these regulations may involve hefty fines. For this reason, if you are thinking of bringing home any plant material, make sure that you obtain information on this subject from the appropriate customs office or plant protection department before setting out. Ask about importation procedures and restrictions and any certificates you might need.

You should also seek such information and permission in the country in which you are travelling. Even once all the appropriate rules and regulations have been observed, there are a few more points to consider.

1. Whenever possible, do not obtain plants from the wild but, instead, ask a gardener at a public or private park if you can buy some seeds or cuttings.

2. Only collect seed in a ripe and dry state. Dry coffee filter papers are excellent for storing and transporting seed. Empty film cartridges are also good.

3. Seeds and cuttings should be labelled with the date and place of harvest and the name of the plant.

4. If you are unable to determine exactly which plant it is on the spot, it is a good idea to take a photograph of a leaf and a flower for later identification.

5. Inform your hotel room service what you are doing so that they do not throw away as rubbish the things you have collected.

6. If possible, take any cuttings as close to your time of departure as possible, wrap them in damp paper and keep them in a plastic bag.

Mostly, it is really not worth the effort of taking cuttings or buying plants to take home because both the travelling involved and the problems of trying to get the plants to grow once you are home will be too great. The safest but also the most time-consuming method is to grow

How plants live

● *Photosynthesis:* A vital green pigment called chlorophyll is contained in the leaves of most plants. During the daytime, due to the effect of sunlight, the plant absorbs carbon dioxide (CO_2) from the air and, with the help of water, processes it into carbohydrates (sugar). Oxygen (O) is a byproduct of this.

● *Assimilation:* With the help of nutrients, the carbohydrates are converted into the building materials of plant life and then conducted to the growth areas of the plant (usually new shoots and tips of shoots) or stored in storage organs.

● *Respiration:* During the night the leaves extract oxygen (O) from the air and release carbon dioxide (CO_2). During this process, some carbohydrates acquired during the daytime are used up.

● *Transpiration:* Under the influence of sunlight and the sun's warmth, plants release moisture via their leaves. This creates a moisture deficiency, which, in turn, causes moisture to be drawn up from below through the plant's roots. If more water is lost through evaporation than the roots are able to replenish, the plant will wilt.

plants from fresh seed. The best alternative of all, however, is to buy the container plants at home and avoid all the hassle!

Points to remember about balcony gardening

It should be perfectly possible to install a large container plant garden on a balcony provided certain rules are observed.

● The strength and structural capabilities of the balcony must be considered. The additional weight created by big containers, plants and other garden furniture should not exceed building regulations; check these with a surveyor, or your landlord if the premises are rented.

● Water, whether used for watering plants or collected as rainwater, should not be allowed to overflow, since it would inconvenience neighbours or pedestrians, or damage the façade of the building.

● If any container plants grow very tall, they should be anchored or staked properly to protect them against the force of the wind.

● You should not undertake alterations to any building, such as installing large frames or espaliers, without first consulting your landlord or other people inhabiting the building. If you are in any doubt, seek expert advice on the situation.

The evergreen, strongly scented
Trachelospermum (left) needs
to be watered and fertilized in
a different way to the profusely
flowering Punica granatum
'Nana' (right). Useful devices for
care are sticky insect tags, granulated fertilizer, a watering can
and a misting/spraying bottle.

Watering and fertilizing

Most mistakes in the care of container gardens are made during watering and fertilizing. Water and nutrients must be supplied at the right time and in the correct quantities if your container plants are to grow strong and produce beautiful flowers. The right pruning method as well as the moderate use of plant protection agents will ensure that your treasured plants enjoy a long life.

Watering and fertilizing

The art of watering

In contrast to indoor plants, which usually enjoy more or less constant conditions, watering large container plants outside is a little more difficult. If you watch them constantly, however, you will soon be able to recognize the signs that indicate that it is time to quench their thirst. Four points should be noted.

1. Sun, rain and wind will greatly influence the time and the frequency of watering.

2. Climate, position and country of origin will supply important information on the general requirements of the species and on when, how much and what kind of water to use.

3. It is necessary to know the degree of hardness of your water and what its pH factor is in order to give your plants the best chance of flourishing.

4. The growth and rest cycles of each particular species will determine when water and fertilizer should be restricted or even stopped altogether.

Hard or soft water?

The calcium content of water dictates its degree of hardness. In general, the following rule will apply: the harder the water, the greater amount of calcium it contains. Calcium is an important nutrient for many plants (see p. 32), but not for plants that are known to dislike chalk or lime. For plants that can tolerate only small amounts of calcium or none at all, a high concentration will often bring about certain death (*Acacia, Acca sellowiana, Arbutus, Callistemon, Tibouchina*). Water that contains calcium can also be harmful to other plants if they have already been supplied with sufficient calcium through compost with added fertilizer, in which case too much calcium will be given if they are constantly watered with calcium-rich water. It is a good idea to find out the degree of hardness of your mains water, which may be subject to considerable regional variation, and to be able to balance the nutrients given to the plant through the amount and type of fertilizer supplied. You can obtain information about your mains water from your local water authority. Even if you use water from your own well or stream, you should still have it analysed for hardness and other substances (ask for advice from your local chemist or garden centre).

The hardness of water is measured in degrees Clark.
● Soft water measures from 0–10 degrees Clark.
● Medium-hard water ranges from 11–20 degrees Clark, which is already too hard for a large number of plants.
● Hard water ranges from 21–38 degrees Clark. Anything above that is very hard.

The pH factor

The pH factor indicates the degree of acidity of a solution or of a particular soil or compost. The pH factor scale extends from 1 to 14. Values between 1 and 6 are acid. The value of 7 is considered to be neutral. Values between 8 and 14 are alkaline (containing calcium or lime).

Most plants prefer soils or water with a pH factor between 5.5 and 7. This corresponds to a slightly acid to neutral reaction (see repotting, p. 56). However, some large container plants have special requirements so it may become necessary to check the pH factor of the water and fertilizer with pH indicator paper, and the pH factor of soil or compost with a special calcium (Ca) detection test (both are available from most chemists or garden centres).

The water requirements of large container plants

Certain factors cause the water requirements of large container plants to vary considerably.
You will have to water more frequently:
● during the main growth phase between the last month of spring and the beginning of the first month of autumn, when the plants are producing plenty of leaves and flowers;

Softening water for plants

Softening agents

If you use chemical water-softening agents (tablets or liquids), the calcium contained in hard water will be deposited as a residue at the bottom of the container after six hours.

Vinegar

Add a few squirts of vinegar to 10 litres (17½ pt) of water in a watering can. This is all right as an emergency measure but use it sparingly.

Peat

Fill a small sack with peat and allow it to hang in a bucket of water; estimate the amount and submersion time according to the hardness and quantity of your mains water.

Further information can be found on pages 30–31.

- in a position fully exposed to sunlight or wind, as evaporation is then accelerated;
- in great heat with little rain;
- in a conservatory, because such enclosed spaces cause lower humidity and higher temperatures;
- plants in pots made of clay or terracotta, as these materials absorb water and lose it again through evaporation;
- plants in small pots, as the volume of compost will not store enough water;
- plants with inferior compost (too much peat or loam), as they dry out too quickly (change the type of compost when you next repot the plant, see p. 56);
- plants that require more than the usual amounts of water and fertilizer, for example *Anisodontea, Brugmansia, Cestrum, Iochroma, Lantana, Solanum rantonnetii.*

You will be able to water less frequently:

- during the rest period of the plant, usually in winter;
- at the start of the growing period, around the beginning of spring up to the second month of spring;
- plants that are positioned in a shady place or sheltered from the wind;
- plants in plastic pots;
- in cool or rainy weather;
- if suitable underplanting is present;
- plant containers that are sunk into the ground.

Our tip: To save too much watering, plant pots can be placed in pot holders made of plastic or in large clay or terracotta containers sunk into the soil in the garden.

Natural protection: Some species of container plants have developed their own protective mechanism to guard against high rates of evaporation or cool temperatures at night. When the sun becomes too strong, some plants actually turn their foliage down. Other plants fold up their leaves. The effect is to expose less of the surface of the leaves to the sun and thus decrease evaporation, e.g. *Acacia, Calliandra* and *Senna.*

Watering and fertilizing

How to water

Watering by hand is still the best method of all. Even the most perfect technology cannot adjust to the individual requirements of plants as well as human sensitivity and judgement combined with the gardener's experience. In large nurseries, of course, where constant conditions are required for the same types of plants, all of this is often regulated by a computer. If you wish to be really good to your plants, however, you should continue watering them by hand.

Automatic watering: Large container plants have to be watered regularly and thoroughly, since the compost in the container will dry out much more quickly than the soil in a garden. Watering aids can take your place for a weekend or during a slightly longer absence (see right). Various different irrigation systems are available in garden centres for these purposes; they can be semi-automatic or even fully automatic. However, these systems are only useful for large container plants if they have been planted out in a bed (e.g. in a conservatory, planting trough or garden bed). The cost and effort involved in installation are really worthwhile if the irrigation system can be fitted as a permanent fixture. In the case of individual containers, however, you should still continue to water the plants by hand.

During a holiday absence

There are various ways of guaranteeing a sufficient supply of water:
● plant containers and boxes with water-storage facilities. The water is sucked out of a tank under the double floor of the plant container (see containers, p. 57);
● watering via an interfacing fabric or felt mat; the mat absorbs water from a storage container. The wick must not be allowed to loop downwards.
● ceramic cones that supply the plants with water. They are also suitable for long-term irrigation. Most systems, however, will only function for a few days. Find out all about it before buying any system and then try it out on one plant before equipping all your containers with it.

Plant sitters: The best method is still to ask a knowledgeable friend or neighbour to help out while you are away. To reduce problems to a minimum, the following tips may come in useful:
● Group together those plants that need the same amounts of water and make a list of them.
● Discuss the list of plants to be watered with your plant sitter and show him or her all the plants.
● Any "problem plants" can be identified by means of a tag attached to the pot. It is best to dispense with any kind of fertilizing during your period of absence.

Waterlogging

Waterlogging occurs when excess water is left standing in a dish or pot holder. Bad drainage, a lack of drainage holes or compacted compost may be the cause. The water then expels the air pockets between the particles of compost, although the plant desperately needs this air in order to carry out its metabolic processes. Permanently "wet feet" cause the roots of your plant to decay. Beyond a certain point, the plant is no longer viable and will die: a large container plant that has been overwatered is doomed.

How to avoid waterlogging
1. When potting or repotting a plant, place a layer of pot shards, Hortag or even a thin layer of pebbles in the pot to provide good drainage facilities (see pp.54–55). This layer will also provide a stabilizing factor for the pot and prevent it from falling over easily.
2. Water carefully and always remove excess water from dishes or pot holders in good time.
3. During extended periods of heavy rain, temporarily move the plant to a site that is roofed over.
4. Use the right kind of compost (see p.56). Composts with a high peat content will often retain water too long. Ensure the compost is crumbly and, if necessary, mix in some coarse sand to improve permeability.

The pomegranate (Punica granatum 'Nana') is an excellent deciduous container plant. Shown above are the phases of growth that occur from the first to the fourth year of life.

5. Containers with a flat underside should not be placed directly on tiles or stone slabs but should be slightly raised on small stone, wooden or ceramic blocks to ensure that excess water can run away freely.
6. Only use plant containers equipped with drainage holes. If necessary, bore holes in the bottom.

Our tip: If the plant is only temporarily waterlogged, immediate unpotting may help as an emergency measure. Leave the rootstock exposed for a short while so that it can dry off quickly. Then replant it in fresh potting compost.

Watering

When to water

● If you cannot feel any moisture to a depth of 1–2 cm ($^1/_3$–$^3/_4$ in) when pushing a finger into the soil or compost around a plant.

● If a clay pot emits a high note when tapped. The sound should be muffled if the compost is moist enough.

● If the large plant and container are relatively easy to lift.

● Whenever a visual check reveals light-coloured compost (this will vary depending on the type of compost).

● If the compost has started shrinking away from the sides of the pot and the plant is looking limp. In this case, the only remedy may be full submersion in a bath of water.

Our tip: If in doubt, the best way of checking is to remove the rootstock from the pot for a visual check. Very often, the upper layer of compost may have been dried out by wind and sun, while the lower areas of the pot still retain sufficient moisture.

Watering methods

Watering from above is the most frequently used and best method for large container plants. Always pour the water directly on to the compost (not on to the stem or foliage) in order to obtain plenty of penetrating moisture and, in the case of fertilizers, an equal distribution of nutrients.

Watering from below is hardly ever done with large container plants as then the plants have to draw up water from the dish or pot holder underneath the main pot, which is too difficult because of the size of the container and the

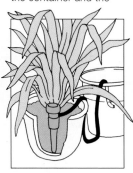

For the holiday season: automatic irrigation using clay cones.

Pour water directly on to the compost; it will then gradually soak down.

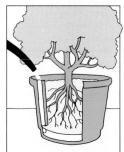

A large container with a specially designed "watering shaft".

volume of compost or soil involved. There is also a danger of water-logging.

Submersion is suitable for plants that have very dense foliage (e.g. ferns) or pots containing a very well-developed root system and not much compost (e.g. *Agapanthus*). This method is also suitable for emergency first aid for plants with dried out rootstocks (e.g. after purchasing, see p. 22). Submerge the pot right up to the base of the stem until no more tiny bubbles are seen to be rising. Then stand the plant in a position where any excess water can quickly drain away.

Giving plants a shower during the summer season will increase

humidity and clean the leaves. Let your plants stand out in a warm summer shower of rain or give them a shower with a gentle stream of water from a hose. Watch out for water-logging.

How to soften hard water

Rainwater is still the best and cheapest kind of water even if it is no longer of the same quality as years ago. Heavy metals, dirt and acid rain may now create a lot of problems for plants. A test with a pH factor indicator may help. Acid rainwater can be mixed with mains water, which, in turn, will become softer.

Our tip: Allow any dirt from the gutter to be washed away before collecting rainwater.

Mains water needs to be treated before using it for watering plants. The following methods can also be employed for larger quantities, e.g. in barrels.

1. Before using mains water for plants, allow it to stand for at least 24 hours. This is sufficient for plants that are less sensitive to calcium.

2. The insertion of special filters in your household water supply system is not cheap but it does provide a permanent solution. It also softens your drinking water.

3. Watering cans with water-softening, renewable filter cartridges are on sale in various sizes. This method is also fairly costly but worthwhile.

4. The use of chemical water-softening agents (tablets or liquids) will cause calcium to collect in the form of a residue, which will accumulate at the bottom of the container after about six hours. They are obtainable from most garden centres or aquarium suppliers. In the case of certain liquid-softening agents, dosing is easy as the solution is mixed with a colour indicator that will change colour from blue to yellow as soon as the right dose has been added. Read the instructions very carefully and follow them meticulously.

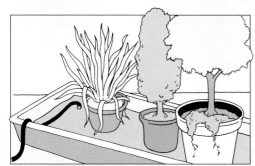

Permeable interfacing fabric coupled with a water-conducting device is ideal for watering a number of plants growing in clay pots for a short period of time.

Ten golden rules when watering

1. Consider any special needs that certain species of plants may have. For example, plants with large leaves present a larger surface for the evaporation of water and will, therefore, require more water.

2. Use tepid water that has been left to stand. Cold water gives the plants a "shock" and interferes with nutrient absorption.

3. Heat, wind and rain should be taken into consideration. The supply of water will last longer in a shady, sheltered position.

4. Do not hold the watering can or hose too high above the plant as this can cause the compost to be washed out and may create watering "holes".

5. A long spout with a fine spray attachment will enable you to reach plants that are set back out of reach.

6. Fill the pot with water right up to the top edge. Allow the water to soak in and repeat until the rootstock is saturated.

If the plant has completely dried out, submerging it will help.

7. Avoid always watering the same place in the pot. A more equal distribution of water will ensure that the compost is moistened through more rapidly.

8. Never water plants in direct, bright sunlight. Drops of water can act as minute magnifying glasses and cause burns. The morning or late afternoon is the best time for watering.

9. Avoid wetting the leaves or flowers. You could end up with unsightly chalk spots on the leaves.

10. Respect the known rest periods of the plant. When the plant is dormant, give just enough water to prevent the rootstock from drying out (see p. 50).

Watering and fertilizing

Bougainvillea (right) adding colour to a patio beside a garden pond.

Plant nutrients

Large container plants require nutrients in order to flourish and remain healthy and strong. Like most other plants, they absorb nutrients along with water through their finest roots or in small quantities through their leaves (see p. 23). Depending on the quantities required, nutrients are used by plants in one of two different ways – as main nutrients or as trace elements.

The main nutrients, which all plants require, are as follows:
● Nitrogen (N) is necessary for encouraging the growth of shoots, leaves and roots.
● Phosphorus (P) encourages the formation of flowers and fruits, makes the tissues firm and helps the plant to grow mature and become woody.

● Potassium (K = Kalium) regulates the water balance and serves to firm up the tissues.
● Calcium (Ca), usually contained in the soil as lime, also strengthens the tissues (see hardness, p. 26).
● Magnesium (Mg) is an important component of chlorophyll and is also essential in the growth process of your container plant.

The trace elements are only required in small amounts. They include boron, iron, manganese, copper and zinc.

Fertilizers

Even in the largest container, a plant will not be able to find enough nutrients indefinitely. It will need added fertilizer. The important prerequisite of a fertilizer is that it should contain all the nutrients required by the plant and in the proper ratios. Years ago, almost the only fertilizer obtainable was standard fertilizer, which was used in greater or lesser concentrations for fertilizing all plants. Nowadays, good compound fertilizers include all the important nutrients but contain them in particular ratios that are adapted to the needs of the individual plant type. The range of fertilizers on offer is vast. There is a wide choice between organic or synthetic, solid or liquid, instant or controlled-release fertilizers.

● *Organic fertilizers* are made out of animal or plant waste matter such as dung, dried blood, horn or bonemeal and other decayed material by the action of micro-organisms. They are absorbed by the roots of plants. The less soil and fewer micro-organisms that are present, the longer the breaking-down process will take. Organic fertilizers are therefore unsuitable for plants with a short growth cycle (from mid- or late spring to mid-autumn, for example).

Our tip: Fruit-bearing plants, such as *Citrus, Eriobotrya, Ficus* and others, are able to absorb manure quite easily.

● *Inorganic (artificial) fertilizer* is produced synthetically and is immediately available to the plant.

● *Liquid fertilizer* can be used immediately and is easy to apply. Add it to water as instructed on the packaging.

● *Fertilizer salts* are dissolved in water before application. As they come in various ideal nutrient ratios, they are very suitable for large container plants and are to be recommended. They are available through the gardening trade but often only in large quantities.

● *Granulated compound fertilizer* can be dissolved in water, sprinkled on the compost or worked in.

● *Fertilizer sticks* are pushed into the compost where they release nutrients when the plant is watered. They are particularly suitable for plants in small pots but not for large container plants.

● *Granulated fertilizer* is composed of tiny granules of fertilizer that have been coated with synthetic resin. It is used as controlled-release or long-lasting fertilizer and, depending on the type, lasts for three to six months.

● *Fertilizer cones* are composed of fertilizer granules that have been compressed together into cone shapes. Their composition and use are similar to those of granulated fertilizer.

Our tip: Avoid cheap fertilizers as they often contain more water than nutrients.

Read the packaging!

Every package or container of fertilizer should state the percentage ratio of the three main components, nitrogen, phosphorus and potassium, in the N-P-K formula, the sequence always being the same. For example, 10:28:10 always means 10% nitrogen, 28% phosphorus and 10% potassium, which means that this particular fertilizer strongly emphasizes phosphorus and is used for improved flower formation. If you know the effect of the individual nutrients, you can use fertilizer to achieve the best results.

How to use fertilizers

Large container plants can be supplied with vital nutrients in different ways.

● *Fertilizing the depression in which you will insert the plant:* This is not recommended for plants in a pot or large container, although it can give a boost when starting off plants that are planted out in the summer and which absorb large quantities of nutrients, like *Brugmansia* or *Cestrum.*

● *Controlled-release fertilizer:* This is good for providing a regular stream of nutrients over a long period of time. It is suitable for large container plants if it is not employed for longer than four to five months. Subsequently, it should be complemented with a follow-up top fertilizer (see below). Granulated fertilizer or granulated compound fertilizer is easy to work into the compost in the pot or can be mixed into the compost when repotting. Press fertilizer cones into the compost along the edges of the pot. Do not use these for plants that are repotted several times a year, as overfertilizing may occur if the compost manufacturer has already supplied fertilizer with the compost.

● *Top fertilizing:* This is the simplest and most frequently used method of fertilizing. Mix the fertilizer with water and pour it straight on to the compost

around the rootstock of the plant (see preparing fertilizer solutions).

● *Leaf fertilizing:* The fertilizer solution is sprayed directly on to the leaves of the plants, using a spray bottle. This serves to strengthen the leaves and the plant during the first few weeks after it starts shooting, as it instantly supplies nutrients to the plant through its leaves. It can be used for all large container plants, even young plants.

NB: Use this method preferably in mid- or late spring. Choose a spray bottle (1–5 litres/1½–9 pt) with a fine-spray nozzle. Ensure that you clean it out thoroughly after use. Use only half of the concentration of fertilizer solution that you would use for top fertilizing. Follow the instructions carefully, otherwise you may find that the leaves become damaged. Spray during the morning or late afternoon, never in bright sunlight, before or after rain or in strong wind. Any residue on the leaves should not be washed off immediately, to give the plant enough time to absorb the nutrients. Do not wash down the leaves until the next time you water the plants.

When to fertilize

Begin to fertilize at the right time using the correct concentration, then nothing should go wrong. Fertilizing time slots during the course of the year are:

● the middle of the first month of spring, when plant growth needs to be encouraged. Start with a half-concentration of nitrogen-rich fertilizer;

● the beginning of the last month of spring, when the plant will have enough foliage to absorb nutrients and process them. Fertilize the plant using the normal concentration, also work in controlled-release fertilizer and begin the first fertilizing of the leaves;

● throughout the summer, fertilize with phosphorus-rich fertilizer to encourage flower formation;

● in summer, fertilize once weekly with a 1–2% solution (2% for nutrient-hungry plants) or fortnightly with 2–3% solution, all depending on the species and constitution of the plant.

Preparing fertilizer solutions

If you have to care for many large container plants, it is worth preparing large quantities of ready-made solution to be kept in a barrel for top fertilizing, or to use a concentrated solution that is diluted as required with the help of measuring jugs.

Ready-made solution
This involves mixing liquid concentrate or salts with the amount of water stipulated by the manufacturer and keeping it in a watering can or barrel. The size of the barrel should be

Tips on fertilizing

● Never fertilize a dry root-stock. This would cause the fertilizer solution to be distributed unevenly and might also burn the roots.

● Never allow well-fertilized plants to dry out.

● Pour the fertilizer solution all the way round the rootstock so that it is evenly distributed.

● Avoid wetting the plant with the fertilizer solution, except when fertilizing the leaves.

● Plants which have been freshly potted in ready-made compost should not be fertilized for at least two weeks as the compost will already contain enough fertilizer for the plant.

● Large container plants with normal nutrient requirements should be fertilized fortnightly (nutrient-hungry plants every week) with the prescribed concentration.

● When using controlled-release fertilizer, keep the compost evenly moist so that the nutrients dissolve properly.

● Cease fertilizing by the end of the last month of summer at the latest so that the wood can mature. Never fertilize in winter.

● Only fertilize winter-flowering plants normally until they have finished flowering. After that, allow a rest period of about four weeks.

● As a rule, it is better to fertilize less often than too frequently.

obtained in 1 kg/2 lb tins in garden centres and nurseries) to 1 litre water ($1^{3}/_{4}$ pt).

● For flowering and growing fertilizer: add 50 g ($1^{3}/_{4}$ oz) granulated compound fertilizer, N-P-K 12:12:17 to 1 litre ($1^{3}/_{4}$ pt) water. Stir the solution vigorously until the granules or salts are completely dissolved and then fill a clean, clearly labelled bottle with the solution. Keep it in a cool, dark place away from children and animals. Shake the solution vigorously before use so that any salts that are deposited at the bottom of the container will dissolve. Combine the correct amount of concentrate with water, according to the manufacturer's instructions, in a watering can or barrel.

chosen according to the number and fertilizing needs of your plants and you should not prepare more solution than will be needed for two lots of fertilizing. Stand the barrel in a shady position and place a lid on top. Make sure that children or pets will not have access to it. Mark the barrel as containing fertilizer if another one with ordinary water in it is standing close by. Before using the solution, give it a vigorous stir so that any residue (particularly in the case of salts) is completely dissolved.

Our tip: For nutrient-hungry plants, apply a handful of

granules dissolved in 10 litres ($17^{1}/_{2}$ pt) water.

Concentrated solution
This requires making your own concentrated fertilizer solution out of solid fertilizer (salts or granules) in a small amount of water. This very concentrated solution does not take up so much room (particularly suitable for balcony gardeners) and is cheaper than ready-made concentrates, which are often not available in the required doses anyway.

● For example, for flowering fertilizer: add 150 g ($5^{1}/_{4}$ oz) fertilizer, N-P-K 8:12:24 (can be

Overfertilizing

A sure symptom of overfertilizing is the falling of green leaves.

First aid

Remove the plant from its pot and carefully loosen the rootstock. Cut back the dead, blackened roots until you reach healthy tissue. Repot the plant in fresh, fertilizer-free compost and water sparingly. Choose a position that is sheltered from the wind and not exposed to bright sunlight. Wait until new roots have formed and have grown well into the compost, then repot the plant.

Common pests and diseases

The wrong position and mistakes in care are often the cause of disease or infestation with pests. If the air is too dry and too warm, scale insects, mealy bugs, spider mites and white fly will start appearing. Lack of proper light, too much humidity and bad ventilation, particularly in winter quarters, will provide a fertile ground for grey mould. Water containing too much lime is the cause of iron and magnesium deficiency (chlorosis). Other pests, such as vine weevils and their larvae, will attack leaves and roots.

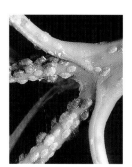

Scale insects

Symptoms: Brown scaly lumps suck the sap out of the undersides of sclerophyllous plants. Large amounts of honeydew secretion render the plant susceptible to sooty mould infestation.

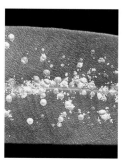

Remedy: Wash off the scale insects with a soap solution. Alternatively, spray the plant with paraffin oil.
Our tip: Take extra care with new shoots. Not all plants can tolerate paraffin.

Aphids

Symptoms: Wrinkled or rolled up leaves and shoots, usually on young growth. The aphids (green or brownish-black) suck the sap from buds and shoot tips and secrete a very sticky liquid, which is an ideal base for fungal infections (see sooty mould). Ants will "herd" the aphids, as they use the honeydew the aphids produce for feeding their young.
Remedy: Wash the plants down with a strong stream of water, then employ useful insects like lacewings (*Chrysopa vulgaris*), ladybird larvae, gall midges, etc. Spray with insecticide.
Our tip: Spray the plants down several times, at weekly intervals, with a soap and spirit solution.

Spider mites

Large container plants are very often infested with red spider mites.
Symptoms: Fine webs that make the leaf undersides look grey. Tiny, light-coloured dots appear on the uppersides of the leaves. The yellowish-red creatures are themselves hardly visible to the naked eye. The leaves gradually turn yellow, dry up and drop off.
Remedy: Employ predatory mites, or use a plant sauna (see p. 38). In very severe cases, use insecticide. Spider mites quickly become resistant.
Prevention: high humidity and good care.
Our tip: Endangered plants should be placed in the correct position right from the start and frequently sprayed with tepid water.

Sooty mould

Symptoms: A black, soot-like layer on the leaves and stalks, caused by a non-parasitic fungus (sooty mould), which, none the less, interferes with the plant's respiration and other processes and makes it look ugly and damaged. Sooty mould will only attack plants that are already covered with honeydew from scale insects or aphids (see facing page). It is not a disease in itself.

Remedy: Wash down or spray infested plants with clear water. Control the pests. Sooty mould is encouraged by dry weather.

Our tip: Check your plants frequently for infestation and take the necessary measures as soon as possible.

Mealy bugs

Symptoms: Small, cotton-wool-like structures, generally situated in the axils of leaves or stems (see photo above), sometimes even around the roots (see photo below). Sticky secretions.

Remedy: As for scale insects. Cotton-wool-like balls should be scraped off or washed off with a soap solution.

Our tip: Isolate new plants for two weeks.

White fly

Symptoms: Small winged insects that sit on the undersides of the leaves suck the sap and excrete sticky honeydew. If the plants are touched, they fly up immediately. The larvae are yellowish-green.

Remedy: Increase humidity and frequently spray the plant with tepid water. Employ ichneumon flies or sticky insect tags. If using insecticides, vary the agent after the second application, since the fly soon becomes resistant.

Our tip: Shake the plant frequently. Susceptible plants, such as *Anisodontea, Asarina, Hibiscus, Mandevilla, Polygala*, or infested plants, should be put in a slightly windy spot.

Grey mould

Symptoms: A grey covering of mould on stems and leaves. Later, brown decayed spots. The causes are over-fertilizing with nitrogen, cool, moist weather and plants positioned too close together.

Remedy: Place the plant in a drier, airier place. Never shake it. Remove infested parts at once and destroy them. Use a fungicide in severe cases.

Our tip: Usually, infestation occurs in the plants' winter quarters, so ventilate this space frequently and make sure humidity is low.

Watering and fertilizing

How susceptible to disease and pests are large container plants?

Basically, large container plants are fairly resistant to infestation and are generally able to protect themselves against attack. However, unfavourable conditions can cause diseases and pests to appear. Container plants are particularly susceptible if they live in conservatories and greenhouses, because high temperatures and air that is either too dry or too humid will encourage infestation by certain pests.

Large container plants that are kept outside are less inclined to succumb to pests and diseases, because, as a rule, more natural conditions, such as wind, moist air and rain prevail.

Plant protection

Sticky insect catching tags: The sticky substance will not only trap pests (white fly, *Sciaridae*, scale insects, aphids and thrips) but, unfortunately, useful insects too. None the less, they can be very helpful.

Plant sauna: this provides high humidity to combat spider mites. Water the plant well, spray it with water, pull a transparent plastic bag over the plant, tie this up to be air-tight and leave for a few days.

Why large container plants become diseased

Usually, the cause is mistakes in care.

● *The wrong position:* too little light, dry air or air that is too humid, not enough ventilation.
Remedy: Move the plants to a different position that offers more favourable conditions in terms of light levels, humidity or ventilation.

● *The plants are standing too close together*, often in their winter quarters. Diseases and pests can easily transfer from one plant to another. The air is often too moist or too dry.
Remedy: Place the plants further apart so that they are able to dry off properly after rain or watering.

● *The plants have not been fertilized correctly*. Overfertilizing with nitrogen encourages growth but does not make the plant resistant to pests.
Remedy: Change fertilizing habits (see p. 34).

● *Plants have not been watered properly:* The compost is too wet or too dry. The plant withers and has very little resistance to pests.

Remedy: Keep the compost evenly moist; submerge the plant in water (see illustration, p. 31).

● *Infection:* New plants were not checked for infestation and were able to infect healthy ones.
Remedy: Watch new plants carefully for 8–14 days (see p. 22). Sick plants should always be kept away from other plants. This will give them a chance to recover without, at the same time, infecting other plants.

● *Chlorosis (mineral deficiency):* The water or compost contains too much lime. The leaves become yellow; the veins remain green.

Remedy: Make the water softer; give the plant a preparation containing minerals.

Increasing the plants' immunity

● Choose the right position for the plant.
● Protect the plant from too much sun and rain.
● Make sure the plant receives a properly calculated, well-balanced supply of nutrients.
● Water evenly. If you check your plants regularly, you will be able to take rapid and successful measures against any infestation by pests and will also halt their spread.

Practical measures
In mild cases, simple methods may help, such as:
● picking off all the pests by hand and washing or spraying the affected leaves with a stream of water;
● increasing humidity;
● cutting off infested or diseased parts of the plants.

Biological methods
Protecting plants with natural methods is healthier for humans and the environment.
● Useful insects, which are the natural enemies of the pests, can be employed. Their eggs are attached to little cards or leaves, which can be obtained through the specialist gardening trade. These cards are hung up among the infested plants. Their effect

will only become obvious after the larvae have hatched but, in the case of severe infestation, this will often be too late. Their use under glass, i.e. in greenhouses or conservatories, is usually more successful as the insects are then provided with better conditions for reproduction than outside in cool temperatures, wind, rain, etc. Lacewings and predatory gall midges are helpful in destroying aphids; ichneumon flies will prey on white fly; Australian ladybirds (*Cryptolaemus montrouzieri*) are excellent for use against mealy bugs; predatory mites are used against spider mites and nematodes are used to get rid of *Sciaridae* and the larvae of the vine weevil.

● Plant extracts made from wild plants, whether brewed as a "tea" or as a fermented solution, will strengthen plants and help to increase their immunity. If infestation is severe, however, their success is often diminished. Frequent use may, in fact, lead to damaged plants. If you have few plants with only a slight infestation, however, you can always try this method.

● Substances containing pyrethrum can be sprayed on all biting and sucking insects. These agents are made from an extract from the flowers of *Tanacetum cinerariifolium* and can be obtained through the gardening trade. Pyrethrum must be handled with care as it is toxic to

humans and animals if the substance is able to penetrate an open wound or enters the bloodstream via damaged skin. Wear gloves. Never use it in the vicinity of ponds, rivers or aquariums.
● Soap and spirit solutions are particularly helpful against aphids and scale insects.
Recipe: Dissolve 1 tbsp liquid soft soap in 1 litre (1¾ pt) lukewarm water and add 1 tbsp white spirit. Spray the infested plants three times at intervals of three days.
● Agents containing oil are based on paraffin. They are considered non-toxic and are successfully employed in sprays to combat scale insects. The film of oil coats the insects so that they can no longer breathe and will die. However, use these sprays only with sclerophyllous plants and never while a plant is forming young shoots.

Chemical agents
The use of these plant protection agents is increasingly being questioned, and rightly so, as they are usually extremely toxic and harmful to the environment. You should only use them in cases of massive infestation, otherwise it is the equivalent of taking a sledgehammer to crack a nut! If possible, choose the least toxic agents and follow the manufacturer's instructions meticulously (see Authors' note, p. 64).

A symphony of colour

Plants from all around the world are seen growing here in a flood of light on a warm summer patio. *Fremontodendron* is an immigrant from California, the bougainvillea and perennial night shade (*Solanum jasminoides*) originate in South America, while the *Aucuba japonica* and lemon tree (*Citrus limon*) have come from South East Asia. One European outsider has slipped in among the exotic foreigners: the pretty blue-flowering *Campanula poscharskyana* is native to the Balkans.

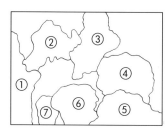

1. *Fremontodendron californicum*
2. *Bougainvillea glabra*
3. *Citrus limon* (lemon)
4. *Aucuba japonica*
5. *Petunia Surfinia* series hybrid with *Plectranthus*
6. *Solanum jasminoides* (perennial nightshade)
7. *Campanula poscharskyana* (bellflower)

Watering and fertilizing

The importance of pruning

Often, the very thought of pruning makes container plant gardeners shudder. Simply out of fear of damaging the plant or losing the profusion of flowers, they often seriously neglect this important part of plant care. Large container plants that are not regularly cut back will grow lanky or become bare, grow too tall or become unattractive; some species even flower less.

Different pruning methods

Cutting back to "open up" a plant and cutting back old wood are the two most important ways of pruning a large container plant (see illustration). Cutting back is particularly helpful for those plants that naturally tend towards leggy growth, e.g. *Acacia, Fremontodendron, Sesbania, Solanum wendlandii, Sutherlandia*.

Our tip: Cut these plants back vigorously in late winter or after the main flowering time.

Cutting out shoot tips: You will obtain a better branching out shape if you pinch out the soft tips of shoots with your fingernails during the summer. This will tend to delay flowering time slightly or even prevent flowering at all during that year, but the compact growth that will result

Cutting back

Cutting back in the usual way removes dried up and dead wood and shortens shoots that have grown too long (see illustration). This encourages the new growth of shoots and the development of compact growth. This form of pruning is helpful with plants that have a tendency to grow leggy.

When cutting back to "open up" the plant, the branches that grow towards the centre are cut out so that light and air can reach the inner parts of the plant and it will no longer grow bare from the centre. This measure is nearly always necessary in the case of deciduous plants.

will guarantee a profusion of flowers in the following year.

The right way to cut back
● Always cut above the base of leaves that are growing outwards. This will ensure that the new shoots also grow outwards.
● Make clean cuts to avoid tearing or damaging the bark.
● Treat the cut surface (if larger than one finger's width) with a wound-sealing preparation

(obtainable in the gardening trade) to prevent penetration by bacteria, etc. that could cause disease.

Our tip: Plants that tend to become bare from below will start producing shoots from the lower buds again after a proper pruning.

How much should be cut back?

This will depend entirely on the plant species and no generalized statements can be made. The best plan is to enquire at the time of purchase and also to check up in specialist literature about each species.

When to cut back?

The right time will depend on the type of pruning cut and its purpose. The main pruning should take place in late winter or early spring (from the end of the second month of winter until the beginning of the first month of spring). In the autumn, you should only cut back as much of the plant as is necessary to make it fit comfortably in its winter quarters. This is because the point at which the plant has been cut will continue to dry up during the winter (see Pruning before moving, p. 49).

Our tip: You may cut back plants such as *Anisodontea, Plumbago, Solanum rantonnetii* and *Tecoma* all year round as this will encourage them to form new flowers. Plants such as *Erythrina* and *Duranta*, which flower at the tips of their shoots, should be cut back before they begin to shoot.

The proper tools

A good pair of secateurs will be sufficent. It is worth investing in secateurs made by a reputable manufacturer as you may be able to obtain spare parts for them for years afterwards. A cheap pair of secateurs will tend to create problems, ranging from blunt blades to blades that tend to break off when cutting tough wood. There are usually no spare blades for these types of secateurs and, if there are, they tend to be more expensive than the original tool! Thicker branches should be removed with the help of a saw. Never cut branches with a serrated knife, as this would cause fraying at the point of cut and other damage that would encourage infestation by fungal infections.

A shaping or training cut

This type of cut, which can be carried out all year round, is intended to give the plant a particular shape which it might not possess naturally. You will need patience and persistence. Species that are suitable for this type of shaping include *Anisodontea, Lantana, Leptospermum, Myrtus, Solanum* and *Tecoma,* which can all be cut into the shapes of cones, globes or pyramids.

How to shape a standard

As standards are often very expensive to buy, gardeners frequently like to create their own. You will, however, need patience if you wish to train a young plant into a successful standard shape.

1. Preferably choose a straight young plant with one shoot.
2. Provide the plant with a support stick and tie it firmly. Make sure the top pair of leaves is not broken off as this would cause premature branching out.
3. Continue carefully pinching out the beginnings of lateral shoots and flowers until the plant has attained the desired height. Do not remove any leaves along the stem, otherwise the plant will not have sufficient leaf surface area for the metabolic processes that are particularly necessary for the thickening of the stem.
4. Do not overfertilize as the wood will then not mature properly and the stem may be in danger of snapping.
5. When the right height has been attained, pinch out the tip.
6. Tie the stem firmly to the support stick beneath the crown.
7. Any lateral shoots that now form should be pinched out after every second pair of leaves. This will encourage the lateral shoots to produce an increasing number of new lateral shoots, soon forming an attractive, compact crown on the tree. Carry on in this way until the desired shape has been attained.

The compost around a Citrus often contains a lot of lime. The matted rootstock of the Correa may make it necessary to repot in early spring.

Overwintering and repotting

The right winter quarters are vital for exotic plants that are accustomed to a warm climate. When the new season begins again, repotting will provide the necessary conditions for the healthy development of your large container plants.

Overwintering and repotting

Evergreen large container plants (cool overwintering)

Name	Temperature	Light	Watering	Name	Temperature	Light	Watering
Acacia	5–12° C/41–54° F	bright	medium (K)	Lagunaria	0–8° C/32–46° F	bright	sparingly
Acca sell.	5–12° C/41–54° F	bright	medium (K)	Lapageria ros.	0–8° C/32–46° F	bright	sparingly
Agave americ.	5–12° C/41–54° F	bright	none	Laurus nobilis	0–8° C/32–46° F	bright	sparingly
Anisodontea cap.	5–12° C/41–54° F	bright	sparingly	Leptospermum	0–8° C/32–46° F	bright	medium (K)
Arbutus unedo	0–8° C/32–46° F	bright	sparingly (K)	Mandevilla ama.	12–20° C/54–68° F	bright	sparingly
Argyranthemum fr.	5–12° C/41–54° F	bright	sparingly	Metrosideros	5–12° C/41–54° F	bright	medium (K)
Asarina erub.	5–12° C/41–54° F	bright	sparingly	Nandina dom. ☠	0–8° C/32–46° F	bright	medium
Calliandra tw.	5–12° /41–54° F	bright	sparingly	Nerium olean. ☠	0–8° C/32–46° F	bright	sparingly
Callistemon	0–8° C/32–46° F	bright	sparingly (K)	Olea europaea	0–8° C/32–46° F	bright	sparingly
Ceratonia sil.	5–12° C/41–54° F	bright	sparingly	Pandorea jasm.	5–12° C/41–54° F	bright	sparingly
Chamaerops	5–12° C/41–54° F	bright	sparingly	Parkinsonia ac.	5–12° C/41–54° F	bright	sparingly
Choisya tern.	0–8° C/32–46° F	bright	sparingly (K)	Passiflora	5–20° C/41–54° F	bright	medium
Citrus species	5–10° C/41–50° F	bright	sparingly (K)	Phoenix can.	5–10° C/41–50° F	bright	sparingly
Clianthus pun.	5–12° C/41–54° F	bright	sparingly	Pittosporum	0–8° C/32–46° F	bright	sparingly
Corokia	0–8° C/32–46° F	bright	sparingly	Polygala myrt.	5–12° C/41–54° F	bright	sparingly
Correa	5–12° C/41–54° F	bright	medium	Sollya hetero.	5–12° C/41–54° F	bright	medium
Eriobotrya jap.	0–8° C/32–46° F	bright	medium	Strelitzia reg.	5–12° C/41–54° F	bright	sparingly
Fremontodend.	0–8° C/32–46° F	bright	none	Tibouchina urv.	5–12° C/41–54° F	bright	medium (K)
Hardenbergia	5–12° C/41–54° F	bright	medium	Trachelosperm.	0–8° C/32–46° F	bright	sparingly
Hisbiscus rosa-s.	12–20° C/54–68° F	bright	frequently	Trachycarpus	0–8° C/32–46° F	bright	sparingly
Homalocladium	5–12° C/41–54° F	bright	sparingly	Viburnum tinus	0–8° C/32–46° F	bright	medium
Kennedia	5–12° C/41–54° F	bright	sparingly	Washingtonia	5–8° C/41–46° F	bright	sparingly

☠ = warning: the plant or part of the plant is toxic; (K) = plants that dislike lime or chalk; l–s = less bright to shady.

Pests and diseases
- Red spider mites: *Acacia, Acca, Anisodontea, Chamaerops, Choisya, Citrus, Clianthus, Hardenbergia, Parkinsonia, Phoenix, Pittosporum, Polygala, Sollya, Trachycarpus.*
- Scale insects, aphids, mealy bugs: *Acacia, Agave, Arbutus, Argyranthemum, Citrus, Eriobotrya, Hibiscus, Lapageria, Laurus, Mandevilla, Nerium, Pandorea, Trachycarpus.*
- White fly: *Anisodontea, Asarina, Hibiscus, Mandevilla, Polygala.*
- Mildew: *Homalocladium.*

Temperature guide for moving plants for the winter
(Short frost only – the rootstock must not be allowed to freeze right through.)
- Plants that can cope with frost to –5° C (23° F): *Acacia, Acca, Arbutus, Callistemon, Corokia, Eriobotrya, Fremontodendron, Lagunaria, Lapageria, Leptospermum, Nerium, Pittosporum.*
- Plants that can cope with frost to a maximum of –10° C (14° F): *Choisya, Laurus, Olea, Trachelospermum.*
- In mild regions, partially hardy plants include: *Nandina, Trachycarpus, Viburnum tinus.*

Note on care:
Check evergreen plants frequently for pests.

Deciduous large container plants (cool overwintering)

Name	Temperature	Light	Watering	Name	Temperature	Light	Watering
Abutilon	0–20° C/32–68° F	l-s	sparingly	Grevillea	5–12° C/41–54° F	bright	sparingly (K)
Acnistus austr.	5–12° C/41–54° F	l-s	sparingly	Indigofera het.	0–8° C/32–46° F	l-s	sparingly
Agapanthus	0–8° C/32–46° F	l-s	none	Iochroma	5–12° C/41–54° F	l-s	sparingly
Albizia jubil.	0–8° C /32–46° F	bright	none	Jacaranda mi.	5–12° C/41–54° F	bright	sparingly
Araujia	5–12° C/41–54° F	bright	sparingly	Juanulloa ☠	5–12° C/41–54° F	bright	none
Asclepias curr.	5–12° C/41–54° F	bright	none	Lagerstroemia	0–8° C/32–46° F	l-s	none
Bauhinia	5–12° C/41–54° F	bright	sparingly	Lantana hybr. ☠	5–12° C/41–54° F	bright	sparingly
Bougainvillea	5–12° C/41–54° F	bright	none	Leonotis leo.	0–8° C/32–46° F	l-s	none
Brugmansia ☠	5–12° C/41–54° F	l-s	sparingly	Leucaena gl.	0–8° C/32–46° F	bright	none
Caesalpina gil.	0–8° C/32–46° F	l-s	none	Malvaviscus	5–12° C/41–54° F	bright	sparingly
Campsis radic.	0–8° C/32–46° F	l-s	sparingly	Mandevilla laxa ☠	5–12° C/41–54° F	l-s	none
Senna corymb.	5–12° C/41–54° F	l-s	sparingly	Melia azedar. ☠	0–8° C/32–46° F	l-s	sparingly
Ceratostigma	5–12° C/41–54° F	bright	none	Montanoa bi.	5–12° C/41–54 F	bright	sparingly
Cestrum ☠	5–12° C /41–54° F	l-s	sparingly	Nicotiana gl. ☠	5–12° C/41–54° F	bright	sparingly
Clerodendrum	5–12° C/41–54° F	bright	none	Plumbago aur.	5–12° C/41–54° F	l-s	sparingly
Cyphomandra	5–12° C/41–54° F	l-s	sparingly	Podranea ric.	5–12° C/41–54° F	l-s	none
Diospyros k.	0–8° C/32–46° F	l-s	sparingly	Poncirus	0–8° C/32–46° F	l-s	sparingly
Dregea sinensis	0–8° C/32–46° F	bright	none	Punica gran.	0–8° C/32–46° F	l-s	none
Duranta rep.	5–12° C/41–54° F	bright	sparingly	Sesbania tri.	0–8° C/32–46° F	l-s	none
Erythrina	5–10° C /41–50° F	l-s	none	Solanum ☠	5–12° C/41–54° F	l-s	sparingly
Ficus carica	0–8° C/32–46° F	l-s	sparingly	Tecoma cap.	5–12° C/41–54° F	bright	sparingly
Fuchsia	5–10° C/41–50° F	l-s	sparingly	Tecoma stans	5–12 C/1–54° F	bright	sparingly

(K) = plants which dislike lime or chalk   l-s = less bright to shady

(K) = plants which dislike lime or chalk   l-s = less bright to shady

Pests and diseases
● Red spider mites: *Asclepias, Bauhinia, Ficus, Cestrum, Diospyros, Dregea, Erythrina, Juanulloa, Leonotis, Sesbania, Solanum.*
● White fly: *Abutilon, Acnistus,* all *Cestrum, Cyphomandra, Duranta, Fuchsia, Iochroma, Malvaviscus, Mandevilla, Montanoa, Nicotiana, Solanum.*
● Scale insects, aphids: *Bauhinia, Bougainvillea, Brugmansia, Cyphomandra, Juanulloa, Lagerstroemia,* the fresh shoots of *Melia, Podranea* and *Tecoma.*

Temperature guide for moving plants for the winter
(Short frost only – the rootstock must not be allowed to freeze right through.)
● Plants which can cope with frost to –5° C (23° F): *Abutilon, Albizia julibrissin, Caesalpinia gillesii, Diospyros, Dregea, Lagerstroemia, Leonotis, Melia, Plumbago, Punica, Senna corymbosa.*
● In mild climates partially hardy plants include: *Campsis, Ficus carica, Indigofera, Poncirus.*

Tip on care: The lower the temperature in the winter quarters, the less watering is needed.

An attractive blend of colours: Acacia armata, Cytisus racemosus and Jacobinia pauciflora.

Hardy container plants

Most large container plants are not hardy in temperate climates, which means that we have to overwinter the plants in frost-free conditions. A very few species can, however, manage to over-winter outside with some protection (see pp. 46–7). Plants described as *frost-resistant or hardy*: When this information is stated on a plant tag or label, it means that the plant is relatively hardy in a temperate climate. Depending on where you live, however, and what sort of winter weather you normally experience, you should still exercise some care.
Partially hardy means that if the plant is given enough winter protection and a sheltered position and if the weather is favourable (not too wet and not much frost), the plant may survive outside. You will still have to decide for yourself whether you wish to test the "hardiness" claim. The safest place is always to move the plant to suitable winter quarters.

When to move the plants to their winter quarters

The right time will depend on the plants' resistance to frost, which means watching your local weather forecasts carefully from the second month of autumn onwards.

Before moving the plants, protect them from excessive rain, so that they are not too wet when moved into their winter quarters. This is important as:
● Excess water will make the pots and compost even heavier.
● Water will no longer be used up so quickly due to the lack of leaf volume, the cool temperatures and the fact that the plants are entering their rest period. Too much water will cause the roots to decay.
Do not move the plants too early
The shorter their sojourn in winter quarters, the better. According to an often-quoted rule, you should move them in from the middle of the second month of autumn and move them out again from the middle of the second month of spring – which might give the plants about six months in a cramped, often dark cellar! No container plant could cope with this without suffering harm in the long term, although most plants are fairly robust and may cope for short periods.
The right sequence
1. When the first night frosts are forecast, move in only those plants that you know are sensitive to low temperatures, e.g. *Bougainvillea, Brugmansia, Carissa, Cestrum, Citrus, Erythrina, Hibiscus, Homalocladium, Iochroma, Lantana, Mandevilla, Musa, Papyrus, Passiflora, Senna didymobotrya, Tibouchina.*

2. All other plants can be left outside as, in general, milder temperatures will follow again. Stand them close to a house wall for protection where, if necessary, they can be covered up with bubble pack, old blankets or large sheets of cardboard.
3. Plants that can cope with a few degrees of frost can be moved in later on (see pp. 46–7).

Pruning before moving

Generally speaking, plants should be cut back before they are moved into their winter quarters, but not too drastically. It will be sufficient to:
● cut back plants so that they will fit into their winter quarters;
● remove dried up, thin or broken twigs;
● cut back evergreens into the desired shape. This reduces the mass of leaves and thereby also evaporation and is a prevention against attack by pests. The final cut should be done before the plants start shooting in spring. You should only cut back rigorously if the plant is very leggy or the species of plant requires it, e.g. *Fuchsia, Lagerstroemia, Lantana, Plumbago* and *Punica.*

Our tip: Do not cut *Brugmansia* back too much as the cut surfaces will dry up considerably during winter. You should prune before the first shoots appear, in early spring.

Over-wintering

Moving the plants inside

● Depending on the situation, prepare heating facilities.
● Light-loving plants should be moved to a windowsill.
● Less light-loving plants can be placed behind these. Plants that are able to overwinter in darkness should be placed in the corner furthest away from the light.
● Do not place any plants too near to the source of heat.
● Polystyrene sheets can be placed underneath the plants so that they do not get "cold feet".
● Do not place the plants too close together as this will encourage infestation by pests or a spread of infection from one plant to another.
● Make sure there is always plenty of ventilation.
● Check the plants once a week for diseases and pests. Fallen leaves should be removed on a regular basis and destroyed.
● Depending on the species and their requirements, water the plants occasionally (see Winter care, pp. 46–7).

Preventing attack by pests

● Hang a few sticky insect-catching tags among the plants as a preventive measure against white fly, *Sciaridae*, aphids and thrips (see illustration, p. 38).
● Check the plants every week.
● Remove any mild infestation of aphids by hand.
● If there is heavy infestation, spray the plants.
● Air the room well on frost-free days. Protect plants that are sensitive to draughts.
● Increase humidity by placing dishes of water among the plants.
● If grey mould develops because the air is too humid, carefully carry away the plants that are infested so that the fungal spores do not infect other plants.

Remove any diseased foliage and spray the plants with a fungicide.

When to water

For large plants in containers, the general rule is the cooler the winter quarters, the less watering is required. Deciduous plants should be kept almost dry; evergreen plants medium moist. The rootstock should never be allowed to dry out.
Do not water at all (cool overwintering): *Erythrina, Fremontodendron, Lagerstroemia, Punica* and *Strelitzia*.
Young plants should always be kept in a slightly warmer place and watered very

sparingly. The same goes for older plants if they are not watered during the winter (*Erythrina, Punica*). Only use tepid water that has been allowed to stand for 24 hours.
Our tip: Young *Erythrina* plants should be watered very sparingly during the winter and kept dry after the stem has become fairly thick at the lower end (after one or two years).

Heating

● An electric radiator filled with oil makes a good frost-guard, particularly if it switches itself on automatically. You can also line the winter quarters with bubble pack to save on heating costs.

Remove withered, yellowing or mouldy leaves immediately.

Regularly remove fallen leaves to prevent decay or mould.

● An emergency solution is an air heater with a thermostat.

● Gas heaters are not recommended because they use too much energy and cause stress to the plants through CO_2 emission.

Our tip: Use a night light with an upside-down clay pot placed over it. The candle will heat the clay pot which, in turn, transfers heat to the surrounding air. This way, plants will easily survive mild frosts for one or two nights in winter quarters.

Additional light

If evergreen plants start losing their leaves, this usually means that they need more light.

Ventilation is important. Provide extra lighting if necessary.

● Neon lights are cheaper to buy and maintain than plant lamps.

● Choose fluorescent tubes with yellow light or a warm colour.

● Only use arc lights in spring or in a warm room, as plants are unable to enter a proper winter rest period with this kind of light, and will carry on growing.

● Screw the lamp to a board and hang it from chains no more than 50 cm (20 in) above the plants. Allow it to burn for 10–12 hours per day (use a timer switch). Maximum use of light will be obtained if a reflector is used. Additional light encourages shooting in early spring and prevents leggy growth.

Transport aids

Large plants in heavy containers are often very difficult to move.

Rollers: Things will be made a lot easier if you move the container around on rollers or castors. Usually, however, the kind of plastic rollers found on sale are not very suitable for use

Rollers make a practical and labour-saving device for moving plants.

on garden paths, etc. so it is often better to make your own.

A trolley is particularly suited to transporting heavy containers up and down steps. It should be stable and equipped with large wheels as well as a collapsible device for standing things on.

Slide: An old trick for negotiating steps is a slide. One or two strong planks can be laid over the steps and the container allowed to slide down them. Hold the container firmly and make sure the planks do not slip.

A porter's trolley will help to transport plants up and down steps.

Our tip: In principle, this kind of transportation should be carried out by two or three people. Use protection when transporting awkwardly shaped or prickly container plants:

● wear protective gloves;

● tie the branches together;

● wrap the plant in a heavy-duty plastic sack or cut-up cardboard boxes and tie this up with string.

Our tip: To prevent branches breaking off, always transport large plants pot first.

Overwintering and repotting

Winter quarters

A heated greenhouse or conservatory makes an excellent winter refuge for container plants. The only problem then is how many plants one can fit in! However, most container gardeners have to make do with emergency quarters and, as long as you observe certain rules, these should be just as suitable for overwintering plants.

The main requirements are:
- they must be frost-free and easy to ventilate;
- they must be as light as possible (if necessary, install additional lighting);
- you must be able to regulate the temperature to suit the species of plants;
- there must be protection from too much intense sunlight.

Greenhouse, conservatory or glass-built extension
The temperature should not drop below 5° C (41° F) at night or rise above 15° C (59° F) in the daytime. Ventilate on sunny, frost-free days but watch out for cold draughts. If necessary, heat the room (see pp. 50–51). Lining the room with bubble pack will reduce heating costs.

Our tip: If in doubt, check the temperature with a mini-max thermometer and adjust the heating accordingly.

Overwintering plants in a house or apartment
In an unheated bedroom or a light, cool hallway, distribute the plants according to their light and temperature requirements. Bring the plants in early enough for them to get used to the different "climate". They will not observe a proper winter rest period because of the warmth. This means watering sparingly and not fertilizing.

Warning: Air that is too warm and dry is very bad for large container plants.

Attic or loft
Choose a space under a dormer window. Protect the plants from frost by means of a framework covered in bubble pack and additional heating.

Garage, extension or shed
Stand the plants close to the window for light and ventilation. If necessary, provide additional light and heating. Partition off the place in which the plants are standing with battens and bubble pack, to save on heating costs.

A cellar entrance or large light shafts above cellar windows
Cover the entrance with bubble pack or something similar. Keep heating facilities handy. Fill the spaces between the plants with straw, screwed-up newspapers or polystyrene to retain warmth. Watch out for mice.

A cool cellar
A cellar makes suitable winter quarters. Do not allow the temperature to rise above 5–10° C (41–50° F) (heating is not necessary). Make sure there is sufficient light (use additional lighting if necessary) and ventilation. Plants that normally live in a cool greenhouse cannot be overwintered in a room containing a central heating boiler.

Overwintering outside

Overwintering outside can be a tricky undertaking because freezing temperatures allow the contents of the pots to freeze right through. Even if you disregard any other frost damage that is happening above ground, this alone will be enough to ensure certain death for the container plant. Planting out the plants will provide a certain measure of protection and in very favourable positions and mild winters (not too wet) this can be tried. Plants that may manage include *Choisya ternata, Ficus carica, Nandina domestica, Passiflora caerulea* and *Viburnum tinus*.

In the garden
1. The plants should be planted out well before you expect any frosts so that they are well rooted in the soil.
2. Place a thick layer of dead leaves, straw or manure over the root area.
3. Protect the plants from intense sunlight and icy winds. Frameworks made of battens and bubble pack or straw mats can be placed over the plants and anchored down well.
4. Provide means for ventilating and shading.

An attractive combination of large container plants: Abutilon, Agapanthus, Solanum and Brugmansia.

A Brugmansia flower.

Our tip: Planting out close to a house wall will provide protection for the plants as well as a means of supporting the frame.

On balconies and patios

1. Stand the containers close to the wall and wrap them in polystyrene or bubble pack.
2. Place a 1 cm (¹/₃ in) thick sheet of polystyrene underneath the container to give protection against cold from below.

3. Do not forget to water on days without frost.

Growth and rest periods

Take growth and rest periods into account when overwintering plants; even subtropical plants have growth and rest cycles. The formation of leaves is often dependent on the length of daylight and not on water supply.

Repotting correctly

When to repot

The best time for repotting is in early spring when you start moving the plants out again. This period should be over by the beginning of the main growth cycle in late spring. Plants should be repotted if:
● the compost in the pot is completely riddled with roots;
● symptoms of deficiency occur in spite of regular fertilizing;
● the compost is old and completely leached of nutrients.
Young plants that are growing fast often need to be repotted several times a year. Choose a new pot that is only one or two sizes larger than the previous one.
Plants that form lots of roots, like *Abutilon, Brugmansia, Cestrum* and *Iochroma*, should be repotted every year.
Very large plants may have a rootstock that becomes too large for the container. When this occurs, it is necessary to take action. Using a sharp knife, cut back around the sides and beneath the rootstock. Add 2–3 cm (³/₄–1 in) of fresh compost all round when repotting.
Exception: Some plants require a narrow pot tightly filled with roots in order to flower better. *Agapanthus*, for example, should not be repotted until the roots are ready to burst the pot or begin to alter the shape of the plastic container.

How to repot

1. Do not water the plant before lifting, as dry compost will make it easier to remove the plant from the pot (see Easy repotting, facing page).
2. Before placing the plant in its new container, water the old rootstock well or submerge it in a water bath. Never repot a dry rootstock.
3. Cut off dead roots with scissors or a knife (do not tear them off), shorten roots that are too long and rough up the matted roots (see illustration).

4. Place a layer of shards, Hortag or pebbles in the bottom of the container for drainage purposes and to stabilize the new container.
5. Insert the plant, and fill all spaces around it carefully with compost, pressing it down gently to firm.
6. Depending on the size of the pot, leave a 1–2 cm (¹/₂–1 in) wide space for watering.

Water the plant but do not start fertilizing again until a fortnight has passed (see How to use fertilizers, p. 34).
7. Do not forget to label the plant. This is particularly important in the case of young plants, which are often less easy to identify than more mature specimens.

1. *Repot when the compost is full of matted roots.*
2. *Remove old roots with a knife.*
3. *Put in a drainage layer and a piece of fabric.*
4. *Insert the plant and fill with fresh compost.*

Thoroughly roughen up the surface of the rootstock with a hand rake.

Drainage

Larger plant containers need a drainage layer to prevent the compost and roots from blocking up the drainage holes. Blocked holes would prevent excess water from running away and are usually the cause of waterlogging.

● First fill the container with a 10 cm (4 in) layer of medium-fine gravel or Hortag.

● Spread a piece of interfacing fabric or slit plastic sheeting (as used for vegetable beds) over the drainage layer and pull it up slightly around the container walls. This fabric layer will prevent clumps of compost from being washed into the drainage layer and eventually blocking the drainage holes.

Easy repotting

Large plants in heavy containers often present problems when they need to be repotted. There are a few ways of making the job a lot easier.

● Leave plants in large containers to dry out for a short while, then the soil will detach itself more easily from the sides of the container. On the other hand, plants in terracotta pots and wooden containers are easier to remove from their containers if they have been watered beforehand.

● A stubborn, tight rootstock can be loosened by laying the plant on its side and tapping the container all the way round.

● You may also slide a long knife around the inside walls of the container to detach the fine roots.

● In the case of very large plants, it is easier if two people tackle the job. One person should

If the rootstock is very matted, use a stone or brick to tap around the outside of the pot; this will make it easier to loosen the plant from the pot.

grasp the plant by the stem and lift it slightly, together with its container. The other person should give the edge of the pot a smart blow with the hand or a piece of wood, a stone or a brick.

Container care

Soaking: Containers made of clay or terracotta should be soaked before they are used for plants. Submerge them until you can no longer see any bubbles rising to the surface. If this job is neglected, the material will rapidly draw moisture from the compost around the roots. More salt or calcium deposits will also appear.

The formation of salts or other deposits on the sides of a clay or terracotta pot need not be thought of as ugly. This is all part of using clay pots. If you still wish to remove the white patches and marks, however, you can place a clay or terracotta container in a bath of water containing a few handfuls of peat for 24 hours. A mixture of water and vinegar in a ratio of 2:1, with a handful of salt added to each litre (1¾ pt) of water will soon get rid of chalk and algae. You can also completely avoid this problem if you place the plant pot in a terracotta container and fill the space between the two with gravel or sand.

Overwintering and repotting

Moving the plants out again

When the frosts are over, you can start moving your plants out again. This time, the sequence is in reverse to the procedure in autumn, which means carrying the least sensitive large container plants outside first.

Before taking them out, check them for any damage sustained during the winter period, cut them back (see p. 42) and remove leggy, overgrown shoots. The plants and their first, delicate foliage will be more sensitive to cold and sunlight after their long winter rest. Some plants will show leaves damaged by sun-scorch at this time. The leaves will soon regenerate, however. If there is a risk of late frosts, proceed with the same measures of protection that you used before moving the plants inside.

Our tip: Large container plants which appear to have died should not be thrown away too hastily. Check first whether there is still some life in the plant:

The nail test: Scratch the rind of the plant in various places with your thumbnail. If the tissue underneath is green, the plant is still alive. Brown or black tissue usually means that it is dead. However, do not throw the plant away before the beginning of the second month of summer, since some plants can regenerate by producing new shoots from their rootstock.

Repotting large container plants

When the plants begin to grow again is the time to repot. Larger containers should be filled with fresh compost. The removal of matted root systems and the right kind of fertilizing are the best ways to get plants off to a good start in the new season.

Planting compost: The range extends from flower compost and your own mixed compost to special composts for certain plants. Specialist literature will give all sorts of directions for use – so what should you do?

Our tip: Nearly all large container plants will flourish without any problems in good flower compost (preferably from a garden centre or nursery). Depending on particular species' requirements, this is a mixture of one part coarse sand and five parts compost. This makes the compost loose and prevents waterlogging.

For plants that prefer an acid compost (pH factor 4.5–5.5), such as *Bougainvillea, Tibouchina* or *Correa,* mix the flower compost with peat in a ratio of 5:2. Using a ready-made compost for "marsh plants" is even simpler; it may also be labelled as ericaceous, rhododendron or azalea compost.

NB: Ready-made compost already contains fertilizer. For this reason, do not add any fertilizer for at least two weeks (see p. 34). You should also avoid using cheap compost from supermarkets as this is often deficient in important components necessary for nourishing the plants and breaking down the fertilizer.

Which container?

Pots and containers are the homes of our large container plants. The plant containers you choose depend on your personal taste and the capacity of your purse.

The cheapest are simple plastic pots and containers. Cement containers with a capacity of 65 litres (14 gal) or 90 litres (20 gal), from the building trade, are recommended for very large plants. These containers have handles for carrying them and are very stable. Do not forget to bore drainage holes to allow water to run off.

The medium price range consists of clay or ceramic containers often imported from Asian countries. Their forms are usually appealing but choose carefully: they often show small flaws in firing and are not always frost-resistant.

The most expensive containers are made of real clay or terracotta and come from Italy, Spain or Portugal. They are beautiful to look at, stand firmly and are absolutely frost resistant.

A Mediterranean patio with herbs and green plants.

In addition, they offer that certain look that makes real Mediterranean containers look so special and reminds us of our holidays in the sun. Pot holders made of plastic or ceramic are better used in conservatories or inside the house as they usually lack drainage holes. Otherwise, you will have to remove water from them after every heavy downpour of rain.

Plastic containers with long-term irrigation systems, which are now offered for sale by some manufacturers, will supply plants with water and nutrients for long periods of time (see p. 28). They are very suitable for large container plants, which can be planted directly into them in the normal way. They can even be made mobile if they are equipped with a set of castors. If you stand them outside, however, rain may create a water surplus. It is recommended, therefore, to bore a hole for drainage at the height of the base plate, above the water reservoir.

Wooden containers never go out of fashion. Wood insulates well and is not as heavy as clay but it does tend to be more susceptible to moisture and weathering.

1

If you act quickly you may be able to save sick plants. Many mistakes in care are easily identified by the appearance of certain symptoms and these can often be reversed or cured.

Fuchsia flower and buds.

First aid for plants

2. A plant that has become waterlogged should be removed from its pot and the rootstock left to dry in the open air. Later, repot it in fresh compost.

3. Water containing a lot of lime tends to form ugly white patches on leaves. Try to avoid wetting the leaves and flowers when watering.

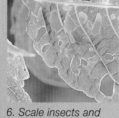

4. Most plants will not die from scorched leaves. Toughen them up after their winter rest.
5. The wrong kind of spray - if in doubt, first try out the agent on one or two of the leaves needing treatment.

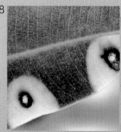

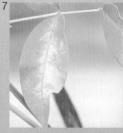

1. Dried up leaf tips indicate that the air is too dry. Raise the humidity by spraying the plant with water. Place dishes of Hortag and water underneath the pots.

6. Scale insects and vine weevils can be collected by hand or sprayed with an insecticide.

7. Spider mites cover the undersides of leaves with gossamer-fine webs. Use insecticides or a plant sauna.

8. Oleander "canker" can be identified by round, yellow-edged spots on leaves, tumorous growth and splitting bark. It is nearly always fatal.

Index

Index

Index